F' nity

EXHAUSTED

SCHOOL

A WARNING TO THE READER

What you are about to read is much more than it appears to be. A junior high school teacher and a former student, now a friend, rented Carnegie Hall with their own money and with their own sweat equity assembled a band of successful schoolpeople to talk directly to an unscreened audience. No college helped, though many were solicited, no newspaper covered the event, though all were notified, no school reformer extended a hand, though most talked of the event privately, urging each other to silence. And yet this first national grassroots speakout on the right and necessity of school choice was a success. Reflecting upon it you will see that it could hardly have been otherwise.

For what was illustrated that evening in November at a world renowned hall was that all of us, you included, have the power to take a hand in national affairs and in the shaping of our institutions. The day of the expert is over, we have seen the universe experts have given us and it is a bad place. Time to wake up. Time to trust ourselves. The *Exhausted School* program showed an unscreened audience what school choice means, but as hard as we tried we could only afford to show a few of the hundreds of sensible ways to grow up. Now it is your turn; you've been warned. If Roland and I could do it, you can, too. A hundred "Exhausted School" programs are needed; build on what we've done, do it better, do it everywhere, and do it yourself without "expert" help. Good Luck.

John Taylor Gatto

THE EXHAUSTED SCHOOL

The First National Grassroots Speakout on the Right to School Choice

Carnegie Hall, New York City

Edited and with an Introduction and Afterword by

John Taylor Gatto

With a Preface by
PATRICK FARENGA

An Odysseus Group Imprint
Smith & Varina
The Oxford Village Press
Oxford • New York

DEDICATIONS

I dedicate this book to my mother, Frances Virginia Zimmer, who taught me how to read by reading to me; and to my father, Andrew, who taught me arithmetic.

I dedicate this book to those people and foundations who made the Carnegie Hall speakout possible:

The Judith Kirsh Kovach Foundation
Ronald Bright Hitchon
The Center for Independent Thought
Andrea Millen Rich
The Josephine Bay Paul Foundation
Fred Bay

and to all those who lent a hand with their time, their money, their voices, their hopes and inspiration, Janet MacAdam, Sue Mojica, Jonathan Rowe, Ron Miller, Pat Montgomery, the Hegeners, the Rodeo Honey people, The United Technologies Corporation, Gene Lehman, Laurie Lee, the Endsleys, the Nishigawas, the Mishoes, Linda Savelo, Dyanne Peterson, Debbie Caldwell, Seth Rockmuller, Katherine Houk, Maggie Smith, John Ohliger, Jack Klenk, Chris Mercogliano, Jerry Mintz, Diana Cohn, Gvuthrune, Linda Lowell, Carmen Wong, Marc Bilgrey, Martin Wallach, The Little Red Schoolhouse, J. Patrick Rooney, and all the others whose spirit has proven indomitable in the face of compulsion and regimentation. When the ugly school empire comes crashing down as it will some day, this brave band will be heroes of that victory.

Sparkle and Shine in the Face of Darkness

Inquiries regarding requests to reprint
The Exhausted School: The First National Grassroots Speakout on the Right to School Choice should be addressed to:

The Odysseus Group
295 East 8th Street, 3W
New York, New York 10009

ISBN USA 0-945700-02-4 Paperback
ISBN USA 0-945700-03-2 Hardcover

Printed in the United States of America on partially recycled paper by The Original Zimmer Printing Company on the Monongahela River. *First Edition 12345678910*

Cover design by Janet MacAdam's Huckleberry Designs
Cover photo by **Jim Graham, SCOTLAND'S FASTEST WING**
Book design by F.E.A. Laser Service, Timonium, Maryland

To order directly from the publisher, add $2.50 to the price for the first copy, 75 cents each additional copy. Send check or money order to:

The Odysseus Group, 295 East 8th Street, 3W, New York, New York 10009

The Odysseus Group is a nonprofit, tax-exempt, public foundation committed to the belief in free choice in education. Opinions expressed in this book do not necessarily represent positions of The Odysseus Group.

TABLE OF CONTENTS

FOR IMMEDIATE RELEASE   October 25, 1991

THE ODYSSEUS GROUP   Telephone: (212) 874-3631
295 East 8th Street   (212) 529-9397
New York, New York 10009

Teacher of Year Calls for Sweeping School Change
Carnegie Hall Rally Demands Free Market Choices in Education

Calling schools and schooling "increasingly irrelevant to the great enterprises of the planet," New York State Teacher of the Year, John Taylor Gatto, announced today his plans for a mass information meeting at Carnegie Hall in New York City for the evening of November 13th. "Schools are parasites on the working community, breeders of social pathology, and the single greatest force working to destroy the American family. That has to stop."

Weaving a close connection between the social pathologies of drug addiction, random violence, and wholesale alienation of the young, the 56-year-old junior high school English teacher, three-time winner of the New York City Teacher of the Year title and the recipient of honors from President Carter, President Ford, and President Reagan spelled out plans for a specific "guerrilla curriculum" to combat the byproducts of dependency he believes are the product of the factory school model.

"I've assembled a compelling program of public, private, and home-school alternatives that should be enlightening to every taxpayer — and hair-raising for the school establishment. We are currently wasting 75 cents out of every school dollar on grotesquely bloated administrative budgets, on phony "coordinators" and an army of other non-teaching teachers, on useless materials, political handouts, and a dozen other boondoggles.

"Come to Carnegie Hall and let me show you beautiful school programs that operate out of mansions on less than one third of what government monopoly schools spend. If we're ever going to see a decent break for young people and families — as well as for the taxpayer — we're going to have to break the monopoly which is guaranteed its customers no matter how badly it does. And let me tell you another thing we're going to have to break: monopoly control of teacher's colleges over teacher certification. The greatest schools in the United States like Exeter, Andover, Groton and Lawrenceville don't use certified teachers — they use anybody their instincts tell them can do the job!"

The Carnegie Hall Program, "The Exhausted School," will feature seven other speakers besides Mr. Gatto, most of them founders of long-running, successful school programs.

Tickets: $5-$30, Carnegie Charge: (212) 247-7800

Preface

by Pat Farenga

> **Everyone knows how to get to Carnegie Hall — you practice. But I never thought of my years of work with John Holt and *Growing Without Schooling* as practice for an engagement at Carnegie Hall, yet in a way they were.**

Everyone knows how to get to Carnegie Hall — you practice. But I never thought of my years of work with John Holt and *Growing Without Schooling* as practice for an engagement at Carnegie Hall, yet in a way they were. When John Gatto first approached me in August about the possibility of speaking at Carnegie Hall, I immediately said "yes," though I had lots of questions.

"Where is the money coming from?" I asked.

"Out of my pocket and Roland's (a student of John's 25 years earlier) and fund-raising efforts," he said.

"You'll go broke! You won't get more than a hundred people to pay to listen to us."

"Don't worry about money; that's my department. This is something I've decided is worth doing. You're underestimating people's need to hear ideas. Audiences listen to me talk for hours on the road, and I'm a lousy speaker. I read from a prepared text. It puzzled me for months until I figured out it's *what* I'm saying that grabs them. People yearn to know *how* we got into this schooling mess. They suspect there are better choices than government schooling. I think the effect of `little people' renting Carnegie Hall and having their say, displaying working options, will build with time. Like the shot heard round the world."

As the evening took shape and more speakers were added to the program, I began to marvel at how the conviction of one man can practically will such a major event into existence in less than 12 weeks. This was not accomplished without difficulty: several famous Teacher Colleges, some unions, a well-known think tank and other groups who didn't like the ideas to be espoused that evening actively worked to sabotage it for several weeks leading up to Carnegie Hall. They almost succeeded. Professional fund-raisers wouldn't work for us because they were told it was "too radical." The State University of New York cancelled two chartered buses set to go. Elements at Bank Street College, Columbia, and Fordham refused to return calls, answer letters, or allow bulletin board postings to remain. John didn't let these setbacks stop him. He told me that in spite of these factors and in spite of having virtually no money, even being $7,000 short of simply paying for the hall a week before the show (!), and in spite of the fact that there were no rehearsals, that some of the participants didn't even know one another, (and some of them cordially disliked one another's ideas), in spite of the fact that we had two 14-year-old boys as masters of ceremonies instead of Bill Moyers (who wrote that he was interested in the event but would be in China at the time)—we drew 1,024 people, as we learned from counting the ticket stubs after it was over.

What an evening! John hired a pianist to play Mozart. He provided a grace note before the show started and during intermission. The men wore tails, the ladies black gowns. Our 14-year-olds wore top hats and looked very natty. Carnegie Hall is actually an intimate space with superb acoustics. From the stage the view is amazing: gold filigree, brass rails, red velvet and mahogany seats are beautifully worked into the hall's design; its multitude of lights gave the effect of a clear sky at night. The hall isn't nearly as deep as it is tall, and the two tiers of box seats and the large balcony above them add considerably to the effect that this is a cathedral for performers. Indeed, after inspecting the hall back in September, John told all of us to practice in large churches to be familiar with the resonance and space we would encounter at Carnegie. My impression of the audience was that a lot of school people showed up in spite of the covert efforts against the show. Teachers, administrators, students, and professors were there, with a number of interested parents, homeschoolers and alternative schoolers, too. There was even a baby in the audience, his gurglings could sometimes be heard clearly and it gave us a smile backstage. Before the event I was told several times by John and Roland that homeschoolers seemed to be the ones supporting the event most. I met Dan and Andy Endsley from the famous Homeschoolers' League of Toledo who travelled from Ohio to be there, and I heard of (though I didn't meet) a group of homeschoolers who travelled all the way up from Florida. Representing homeschooling in such a place, and to an audience that largely had never heard of homeschooling before, was a thrill and honor for me and my family. People came from 17 states in all.

The evening was structured so Victor Gonzalez, a 14-year-old student of John's, was first to face the audience. He provided me with an image of that night I can never forget: we got the cue to start. I saw the large crowd silently waiting in darkness, a single shaft of spotlight appeared, waiting for Victor to walk towards it. I patted Victor on his shoulder, wished him luck, and saw him take a deep breath. Then I saw his little frame, a silhouette in tails and top hat, bravely walk to the podium and open the show. He soon got the audience to laugh exactly where he wanted laughs, and he introduced each speaker flawlessly (as did his counterpart for the second half of the evening, young Jamaal Watson). Both performed with only a few run-throughs about two hours before curtain time because John couldn't afford rehearsal time at $300 an hour. Again, I was shown how capable youngsters can be when they are trusted and treated with respect.

When Victor finished his stint he introduced John — whose role for the evening was to criticize schools. The rest of the speakers were to *avoid* criticizing schools and instead to present as forcefully as we could the unique logics behind our various educational approaches. I spoke next, then came Dan Greenberg (from the Sudbury Valley School near Boston), Kathleen Young (from the Waldorf-inspired Hawthorne Valley Farm School in Duchess County, New York) and then a former student of John's, Roland Legiardi-Laura, who spoke about his adventures in self-education as a filmmaker, poet, and as a self-taught general building contractor.

The second half of the night consisted of Dave Lehman (from the Ithaca Alternative Community School in upstate New York), then another former student of John's, Barbara Jill Cummings, who spoke about her self-education in the field of ecology, teaching herself Portuguese and living in the Amazon to examine the impact of dam-building on the local native cultures, Mary Leue then spoke of her Albany Free School, which owns ten buildings and operates six businesses as part of their "community" curriculum. John closed the evening with a ringing denunciation of government monopoly schooling and a call for alternatives, after which we all retired to the Maestro's dressing room for a reception.

Before we came to Carnegie Hall, John wrote us all, urging that our purpose be to inform and be useful to people who come to hear us. Our long-range purpose was to establish that choices are available and to suggest that no sane decision can be made without knowing what those choices are. That we succeeded in these goals has become apparent to me.

John is using the Carnegie Hall event as a model for presenting local education options in other parts of the country. This spring he will do a similar event in the West, but his real goal is to have everyone and anyone understand that leadership is not the prerogative of an elite.

John recently wrote to me, "We established a model at Carnegie Hall — which can and will be improved upon — but a model whose existence will be slowly heard of, mark my word, because it asks the question — why wasn't this (letting people know about their educational options) done before? And done by those who have the stewardship of our schools?"

By John's example, we see just what can be accomplished, on a grand scale, by just one person. I doubt Carnegie Hall will ever see such an assortment of non-professionals taking over its stage. Which brings me to the second indelible image of that night: the shoes that came with John's tails were too tight for him, so he took them off and did the whole performance in his stocking feet! That was a lesson about free market choice I'll remember for a long time! ◆

Introduction

by John Taylor Gatto

" It's hard to believe that in six weeks, if the breaks go our way, we'll be on stage at Carnegie Hall in what I hope will be only the first of a national outbreak of grass roots speakouts aiming to revive the public discussion... **"**

No, it can't be October 1!

To: B.J. Cummings   Mary Leue
       Roland Legiardi-Laura   Dan Greenberg
       Jamaal M. Watson   Dave Lehman
       Victor Gonzalez   Pat Farenga

From: John Taylor Gatto

Subject: Carnegie Hall, "The Exhausted School"

I.

*I*t's hard to believe that in six weeks, if the breaks go our way, we'll be on stage at Carnegie Hall in what I hope will be only the first of a national outbreak of grass roots speakouts aiming to revive the public discussion — closed down in my own reading of our history in the mid-19th century because of a panic among the elite caused by the Communist Revolutions of 1848 in Europe. It was widely believed the immigrants would bring the infection with them, and for the second and fatal time in 1919 with the national "Red Scare"/Palmer raids hysteria after the Russian Revolution. But whatever the threads of causation, democracy without participation has become the national norm — and that's no democracy at all.

We'll all have our own purposes for participating in "The Exhausted School," but what I just wrote is one of the three major reasons I set time aside out of my own life to try to do this. Another major one, of course, is to take a direct hand in public information about what's *possible* in schooling so that the idea of change is given color and form and doesn't just remain a dead abstraction. In my opinion, *all* the principals in current school reform rhetoric have failed to do this — perhaps it's innate in institutional responses to anything that their designs *exclude* more people than they include, but whatever the case, I believe each one of you knows more about how children and other human beings learn than all the "experts" and titled personages combined.

I want to use this letter to give the evening a shape. In the nature of our lives and my very modest finances there will not be time to get together before early November, perhaps not before the very day of our mutual appearance. The constant running around I have to do to write, disseminate, arrange, publicize, and most of all to fundraise, will make it difficult for us to make contact by phone *through* me (though by all means call each other) or even for me to respond at length to letters. I'll try my best but money, publicity, meeting with sponsors, etc. has to be the overriding concern.

I'll try to address all the issues in which you may have questions. We're divided into two groups: a) five "schoolpeople" who correspond to the various themes noted on the enclosed flyer, *viz.*

"How To Bend the Bars of Our Traditional Factory Schools"

That's me and what I've done for most of my 26 years as a teacher: Work inside the worst schools in New York State (statistically). So I'll take on how to change the unchanging while remaining *inside* — the fate of most kids.

"What Real Public School Alternatives Can Do!"

That's Dave Lehman. And "real" in this context means licensed/ authorized by the current form of school governance *to be different*. Everything I did as a guerrilla teacher was illegal and unauthorized, adversarial, self-financed, and extremely wasteful of time, energy and peace of mind. Systemic change won't come from people like me because few are crazy enough (or angry enough as was my own case) to spend their lives in combat. Dave represents many of the wonderful possibilities that can grow out of a vital plan, an imaginative staff with a sense of itself as a team, and a measure of cooperation from "authorities" — indeed, *trust* might be a more accurate appraisal but that's for Dave to say. His job, *as is everybody's*, is not to speak generically but very specifically, to tell us what his school is, where it is (characterize the community), *and what its own peculiar logic and experiences have been.* Then, and only then, should its "lessons" be abstracted and summarized. The great value each of you represents to a general audience — including to those who *wouldn't* send their kids to a school like yours — is that you are REAL, and that you are doing work that *one segment* of the population finds useful and inspirational.

Your very presence, Dave's, mine, and everyone's, is a testimonial that there is no one right way. There are many ways to grow up solid, sane and satisfied — monopoly schooling has stolen that understanding from our population. We once had it to an amazing degree before the Civil War, for hundreds of years of our history; and that kind of choice appears to be the easiest way to get back on track — *trust* people, kids, parents, communities to pick what's right for them, because if you don't believe *that* you believe that "experts" can do a better job. The last 140 years of one-way compulsion-schooling gives that the lie, I think.

Please, don't anyone "politic" about "what's wrong with American schools" (except peripherally, of course) — your very own success described minutely with lively human illustrations, then its principles summarized at the end, *will be the most powerful political statement of all.* Because you will have demonstrated by your practice that many methods of growing up work just fine, and that they don't cost the taxpayers one extra cent (indeed in Dan, Mary and Pat's experience, they cost *less.)*

I've taken longer on Dave's portion because the points generalize to everyone. Dave has a working public school alternative, approved by the city of Ithaca — it's his job to represent the whole category of this possibility *by representing his own design well* (not by doing a survey of the category).

"Exciting Private School Choices..."

The public perception of private schools created by Exeter, Andover, Lawrenceville, Hill, Choate, Groton is a false one. By preempting the public imagination with a vision of the great classical English boys' schools, the whole canvas of private alternatives — working and as yet undiscovered — is closed to inspection. Furthermore, the idea that private school is expensive and public school is cheap is, of course, managed by a stage trick on the part of the government — of the two forms public school is by far the most expensive in direct cost (we'll leave social costs out of it for the moment!), averaging $5500 a year per seat nationally, to a national average for all forms of private education of about $2200! Some aspect of "school reform" is going to happen when enough people realize that the distinction between public and private is a very shadowy one — all children come from the public and are returned to it. In nations like Holland 90 percent of private school tuition is rebated by the government to anybody who makes a private choice. Whether we should take that path as a country is not the central issue, but whether we should allow a vigorous national discussion and referendum on this *is*. Surveys of our growing underclass population show them heavily in favor of having such a choice — even *without* the necessary national debate. Dan Greenberg and Mary Leue will represent the category of private alternatives by representing their own unique and highly individual communities —

The Sudbury School

The Albany Free School

In my opinion, they should not refer to each other, to NCACS and the history of the alternative movement, and not to any other abstraction that tends to de-emphasize their own private genius. Mary should say what the Albany Free School is, how it came about, what makes it work, what happens to its kids afterwards, (everyone will want to know — can they go to college?!) — in other words what the peculiar logic, the spirit of the place is.

Dan, who has written 116 books (!) should do the same. Because of the spectacular appearance of the campus of Sudbury I wish he could see it in his heart to make an enormous photo blowup of the place — Grand Central size to set on stage. Its grandeur underlines the low cost of admission and would bring a gasp from any audience that wasn't dead. (We *might* be able to show a slide behind him as he speaks — and that is true for all — *if* we get financing...Carnegie has a *stiff* charge for every single service they provide: $150 for a spotlight, $600 for an organ — no player — etc. etc.)

Once again, by representing themselves well through logics that only *abstractly* have much to do with each other, i.e. Sudbury is unmistakably *sui generis*, ditto Albany Free, — the whole range of possibilities will come across dramatically.

"How To Get An Education At Home"

...introducing Pat Farenga, and hopefully a mounted photo blowup of Day, his wife, and the two little Farengettes because Pat will stand there representing 500,000 families (or more) currently homeschooling in the U.S. — up from 10,000 a decade ago — and I guess also representing the many national networks of homeschoolers like Pat Montgomery's Clonlara, the Hegeners, the Colfaxes, *et al.* Furthermore, although I know it may get him assassinated, he also embodies the homeschooling principle that emerges among religious fundamentalists and whose purpose, as I understand it, is to preserve a culture and outlook. In that regard the Amish and Mennonites and other pietest sects are a variant on the theme too, I suppose.

To all of the Carnegie speakers, homeschooling will be a familiar theme, but to all the great bulk of intelligent laymen it is the greatest mystery of all. Do you nail a desk to the kitchen floor and ring a bell in your kid's ears every 40 minutes? Will he learn to talk to other kids? Don't you go crazy hanging out with children all day long? What if it's a one-parent family? Can they get into college? Sure, "smart" people can do it but can we trust "dumb" people to do the same?

Pat, as Pat the homeschooler, and Pat as a close personal friend of John Holt and the bearer of his tradition through *Growing Without Schooling* and his network of homeschooling families is the person the audience will be fascinated with on stage. If he represents himself well, and uses examples from the families he knows directly, he will show unmistakably how unique, how singular, how one-of-a-kind every homeschooling experience is. He will prove conclusively *without saying it* that there is no one right way to do this business of becoming a good human being.

"The Voices of Self-Schooling"

Four speakers on the program represent people who in my estimation — and I watched them all closely as my students in days gone by — had the instinct toward self-schooling which marks those who will become "educated." My belief is that conventional schooling preempts the time we need to keep appointments with our developing selves, critical appointments to learn self-reliance, confidence, skill, family relationships, judgment, and a host of other skills without which we never become fully human. It's my opinion, further, that the multiple dependencies children are inoculated with by compulsion-schooling are one of the principal causes, perhaps *the* principal cause, of the various social epidemics surrounding us in American society: anger, violence, despair, teenage suicide, addiction to narcotic drugs, passivity, envy, divorce, national buying obsessions, *et. al.* are reflections of dependent personalities, made that way by schooling.

But my beliefs aside, all of the four students represent young people who are adaptable, resolute, and know how to use their time. They were not *taught* these things, but they did *learn* them by being given a large diet of raw experience when they were young which provided an opportunity for them to develop. And although my own role in helping their development was only a small fraction of the whole, they represent three progressive stages in my own development as a teacher.

◆

Roland Legiardi-Laura lost his parents as a teenager, had no close relatives within 1000 miles, and had only a very small inheritance, about enough for one year's modest maintenance. Yet he bicycled across the U.S. *alone,* hand-sewing 15 flat tires on the way, lived on a canal boat in Europe for a year, became a professional *poet* and made his living that way (!) for a number of years, taught himself structural engineering, all phases including blueprinting and bidding, and began to make an excellent living that way, taught himself filmmaking and with no prior experience raised hundreds of thousands of dollars, made a film about Nicaragua, and won nine international film awards with it, *and,* in his spare time, opened a night club in the East Village which has become world-renowned because of its original theme.

Without being self-conscious about it, Roland is a master of self-schooling, as Ben Franklin and Andrew Carnegie and Lear of Learjet fame were. Somehow he understood on an unconscious level what an education is, how it differs from schooling, and what experiences are necessary to provide the tools to have one.

Nobody wouldn't want their son or daughter to turn out resourceful, honorable, talented, humane and successful like Roland.

What he did, how he did it, how he sees the world and his place in it, and what school might have done to help him become himself are some of the things he and the other students will explore. Again, like all our speakers, his main force will be spent on exploring himself, not on grand abstractions about what's wrong with schooling.

Roland, besides being my friend and mentor, represents the first stage of my teaching career, one in which I concentrated on these three themes:

a) That my life, my values, my decisions — and the similar attributes of each of my students — our *community* nature, put a different way, was the most important thing I had to teach. Thus, from the beginning it was our individual humanity, not textbook abstractions, that made the foundation of our classes.

b) That adolescence was a junk word, a synthetic construct without value. From the beginning I assumed that my students' minds were capable of any degree of sophistication and so I "pushed" a 13-year-old group into levels of nuance and abstraction that most graduate classes never attain.

c) I *only* taught what I wanted to learn or explore myself — operating on the theory that passion of mind, and its attendant procedures, was the most valuable thing I possessed to transmit, and on the corollary theory that *anything*, including plumbing and knitting, is intricate and fascinating — and broadly instructive — if (and only if) you can be presented it by someone who loves the craft.

Barbara Jill ("B.J.") Cummings was a student of mine 13 years after I had Roland. (She's 24 now for you number crunchers and detectives). By B.J.'s school year I had developed the intense study of each student's life to a genuine passion because I had discovered how much it taught *me* about human possibility and the range of wonderful difference — as various as the human fingerprint — and because it enabled me to individualize my relationship with everybody and invent a private "curriculum" for each.

B.J. was a wonder from the beginning. Though living with her mother on the lip of Harlem (in an area which would have frightened most young people) B.J. was tough-minded, independent, and gutsy from the start. Before the school year was over she had designed an amazing street business to sell handmade creations (scarves, gloves, shawls, etc.) produced by nursing home residents on the streets around Columbia, and had appeared at the night meeting of New York City's fearsome Central Board of Education, booked a speaking slot, and given them Hell for not teaching entrepreneurship to kids. The Board which she flayed gave her a standing ovation and quoted copiously from her speech in a publication sent all around the state.

Seven years later...B.J. took time off college, taught herself Portuguese, *and went to live with the Indian tribes of northern Brazil!!!* Under constant surveillance by government spies (!) she studied the effects of dam-building on the cultures above and below the dams and wrote a sensational analysis, *Dam the Rivers, Damn the People*, which was published when she was 23, in various languages and with the imprimatur of the World Wildlife Foundation.

◆

She also owns a formal black strapless evening dress she intends to wear to Carnegie Hall with long black gloves and is currently a PhD candidate at UCLA.

B.J., as Roland before her, will undertake to show us her own internal path which brought her to young womanhood accomplished, fierce, and ready for anything.

Although she originally wanted to use the Carnegie forum as a platform to explore her interests in political ecology (or politics of ecology is more accurate) she has a much greater gift to give the audience assembled. They are there to find out how people really learn and how the greater community can help them. In my opinion the only people who have been shut out of that discourse are the learners themselves — who know more about it than anyone. With six weeks to analyze her own development, and perhaps to consider how government schooling might have been useful instead of a barrier to be overleaped (if there is such a word); if B.J. hadn't followed the course she did, I think she would have distinguished herself in any other endeavor.

Now...we can either believe conveniently that talent like hers is distributed over a bell curve, or pyramidally like the Egyptians did, (You may have your own opinion on that, but I reject the contention outright based on my own experience. Talent, even genius, is very common, I think), or it is in most all of us and something draws it out. It's B.J.'s challenge to figure out what that was and describe it for us after she details her adventures from 5 to 20.

By the time I had B.J.'s class I had articulated a theory of experience which incorporated the themes I brought to Roland's class, but added seven more categories of experience, each wide enough to support any number of individual designs. Without going into the theory of each particle of the new additions, I believe that each "does a job" that is unique, that something important is lost without one or more of these experiences *gotten early.*

The Seven Themes that B.J.'s Class Got:

1. Community service. The real kind where you go to work with the *paid* employees, and go home when they do. This is opposed to the community service under the tutelage of "nice" people, with milk and cookies, the kind that "decorates" some alternative programs. I expected the kids to shoulder an adult load of responsibility and prove their usefulness to others. All did.

2. Independent Study. The real kind. One boy took 180 days to get a part on "General Hospital" but in the course of doing it he studied acting, directing, lighting, scripting, advertising, the history of theater, the relationship of theater and the academic disciplines of psychology, sociology, history, etc. And, he got paid! One girl

analyzed the public swimming pools of Manhattan and the Outer Boroughs from a professional swimmer's perspective and rated each on the basis of a checklist she had devised, writing "A Swimmer's Guide to Swimming Pools in the New York Metropolitan Area."

3. Apprenticeships. Either "The One Day Apprenticeship" or long-term. The idea: to learn how someone thinks and makes decisions. The purchase price: trading personal services for the right to shadow a person at work.

4. Field Curriculum. In which various parts of the community are studied as living texts and contexts in projects which are semi-independent (although designed by myself) and usually lead to a product of immediate utility. To have a kid furnish a two-and-a-half room Manhattan apartment down to the toothpicks and toilet paper by sallying out for days with a clipboard, and tallying the costs of his selections with tax computations, tabulations and the whole package including architects' drawings, placement, symbolic graphics, etc. is a wildly successful example; analyzing the commercial community of a 50-block area of the West Side in order to direct a part-time job search is another.

5. Parent Partnerships. At *any* time and for *any* family — determined motive, kid and mother, kid and father, kid and granddad, kid and aunt, etc. have the right to "write" a piece of family curriculum and substitute it for the school-authored one. I see now in retrospect that this was my nod to home-schooling and to the absolute centrality (in my own philosophy at least) of the family relation as the basis for a "self," and for the values which produce a successful, happy life.

6. Work/Study. Consider B.J.'s design for a street peddling business in the Columbia/Barnard area using one of a kind, handmade items made by old people. One boy buffed restaurant floors, in a service business of his own design, many have done pet-sitting; the most successful kid I ever had in a dollar sense made $600 a day selling homemade cartoon character stationery at Comic Book Conventions. His mother called me and gave me living Hell for teaching her son how to make so much money at 13 — but, of course, he taught himself! In a work/study program, school time is exchanged for work time as long as the work is self-initiated, a private business launched by the kid, not a "job" to make spending money.

7. Solitude/Privacy/Self-Reliance. This is a complicated idea I

won't spend much time on, but suffice it to say the theme is designed to counteract the hideous *lack* of private space, private time, private thoughts, private business in a government factory school, or most private schools for that matter. I operate on the theory that the formation of a reliable self requires time spent alone in the wells of spirit — and that it is nobody else's business what you do there, store there, think there. With many children crippled by a total surveillance model of schooling, it's necessary to "show them how," to run exercises that *demand* learning to like your own company, keep your own counsel, make your own decisions. Walking the ten miles alone from Columbia University to the Staten Island Ferry might be one of these, going fishing another, but the whole area touched here is vast, subtly nuanced, singular, and a constant struggle.

So, by B.J.'s time with me I was working these themes regularly with a very mixed bag of kids, from school dropouts to kids who scored off the standardized scales — and the mix was evenly divided between both extremes and the middle.

With almost all the experiences, however, John Gatto was the final destination. Each undertaking required some written, verbal, or photographic/graphic documentation, and the "record" thus created became my own passport to the various "titles" I accrued later — though that was not the purpose, of course. In my own mind I still had not broken the tight connection I thought must exist between "student" and "teacher" — it was that aspect which was to change most radically between B.J.'s time and the present, when I began to "teach"...

Victor Gonzalez and Jamaal M. Watson.

My teaching venue changed radically from B.J. to these boys who were students of mine until July, 1991. B.J.'s school was the flagship secondary school of my District, smack in the middle of the Gold Coast of the West Side, dripping with extras, seemingly safe (although three students were raped there during school time over a one-year period, this was unknown to most of the staff/parents). But Victor and Jamaal's school was in the center of Spanish Harlem, had spawned many of the famous Central Park jogger's rapists, was the "scene" of four *different* murders in June of 1990 — two students, two parents — and is one of the 59 lowest rated schools of the thousands in New York State (as of 7/91). Both of the young men had been in serious trouble in the past, one for carrying a gun (dummy) into an elementary school and menacing with it (as well as numerous other peccadilloes); and one for repeated angry encounters with authorities, a hostile manner, and an almost total unwillingness to do class work.

At the end of one school year, the collective production of these two kids in the final version of my "guerrilla curriculum" was as follows:

1. Two first prize ribbons and one second prize award in citywide writing contests competing with other high school kids from Bronx Science, Stuyvesant, and other top high schools.

2. A hard-won weekly apprenticeship with one of America's top comicbook authors, a young woman who herself is a PhD candidate in International Studies at Columbia.

3. Visits to 20 engineering offices for complex presentations by both high level executives and plant workers — including BOAC, the George Washington Bridge, Lincoln Tunnel, The Path Trains, the World Trade Center, and many more.

4. One full day a week excused from school to journey to a private library and undertake a complex, self-guided study of graphic art.

5. Breakfast guests of Senator Bob Kerrey (Nebraska) and movie star Debra Winger (Hollywood!) at the famous Algonquin Hotel where, for three hours, they chatted about the problems of schooling.

6. Jamaal's appearance as the student representative of his school at meetings of the "School Improvement Committee," a job paying $15 an hour.

7. Acceptance at year's end of both boys — heretofore regarded as mildly retarded — into one of the most competitive special high school programs around, one which admits only one of ten applicants, a stiffer ratio than Harvard's.

◆

The biggest change that came over my teaching practice between B.J. and these young men was the realization that *my own* constant surveillance and mediation of student lives *was not* the critical determinant of value in their experience — the only critical thing was the experience itself! For me this understanding has constituted a great breakthrough allowing me to understand Benjamin Franklin and all the great homeschoolers of history. I now believe that the teacher part of the teacher/student relation is wildly overstated, and probably for obvious reasons — it makes the "profession" legitimate, allows intricate career ladders to be built, furnishes fortunes to various school-related industries, creates gurus in profusion, from Piaget to Howard Gardner and Ted Sizer — all the way down to myself. And in various other fashions feathers many a nest.

I've spent much time describing the kids and the parts of my own development they mark partly to explain their presence on the program and partly to offer an insight into the fellow who dreamed the idea up. I now believe the best teacher I ever had was my mother who read to me every day before I was five, so shakily that she had to run her finger under every word to hold the line. By the time I went to first grade I was reading so fluently from that innocent daily practice that the first grade teacher came to our home to complain I was making the other children feel bad. Not phonics, not "whole word", nor any other bogus theory of reading propelled me, just someone reading by my side, day after day. I think we have labored mightily in creating a science of pedagogy and produced a tiny flea. I think further that our problems in schooling are self-created, and largely persist because the apparatus of schooling is profitable and will not surrender its perks easily.

The "kids" are on this program to prove that point even though they may say whatever they please. If they analyze their own accomplishments I rest content it will be obvious to all we are hearing the voices of self-teachers.

Some logistics:

DRESS:

By professional house advice of the Carnegie management the men should appear in tails, the women in black evening dresses ("Mae West's," B.J. calls them). Because of time and other pressures I'll have to leave it to all of you to get fitted for a rental and arrive with it. I will, although the thought makes me shudder, do myself and the two 14-year-old boys. If I don't show up myself November 13, you will know I am pursuing them somewhere through Central Park.

THE HALL:

This is the most impressive room I've ever been in in my life. To stand on stage is to feel your knees weaken. Let me trust all of you to practice your deliveries in some local cathedral. *If financing arrives and we can afford it*, I'll book a rehearsal for the day before, a walk-through so you won't come to it cold — but we must face realistically the possibility this *won't* be affordable, and be prepared. I'll do my best.

TIMING:

Again, this depends largely on how much money I'm able to raise over the next five weeks. If we go one minute over the allotment, the charge is gigantic; if we go 20 minutes over I must move into a tent that very evening. Therefore, each speaker named has 15-16 minutes (the young kids will probably only use 10 between them).

CONTINUITY:

The boys will give each of you a short (one minute or less) intro, and open both halves of the evening. We'll all be in black, the plan now is to darken the stage, have the podium at stage left and one at stage right and a big overhead spot. We get a little drama this way, alternating the location of the speakers. Where the others will be during the speaker's time hasn't been arranged yet but you'll get diagrams, etc. in plenty of time.

MUSIC:

If it can be afforded — again that bugaboo of finding backers — there will be Mozart/Bach from 7:00 to 7:30 (we start sharp!), and at the short intermission, and as the crowd leaves. We have only a short shot at impact and, without theatrics which would jar, I'll try to load as many class touches as can be afforded to the ensemble. People associate school talk with drabness, fatigue, mean-spirits, fussy people usually so I'm aiming for the impact of the best hall in the United States and white tie, Mozart, the chiaroscuro of single speakers spotlighted, etc. to give us what drama we need to avoid just being talking heads.

EXPENSES:

As most of you know the cupboard is bare, and it will take a small miracle to pay for what I've already contracted. The total cost will be 40 to 50 thousand without a PR person, and much more with one. I've established a series of fall-back positions to ensure that the show will go on, even if *we* are the only audience for it, but even assuming (as I most certainly am) that we pack the house, this is probably a break-even, small-loss operation at best — and a bone-crunching loss at worst. NOT TO WORRY! However, unless financing comes through I won't be able to pay your expenses. On the other hand, if it does, I will. Hope that's fair enough. About one half of the tickets in the house will be freebies, perhaps more, in an attempt to attract press and other people (politicians) who need to hear what choices *are already out there working*. I won't know what's happening until a few days before the show in a financial way — and that is compounded by the natural fact that most people don't buy tickets to a thing like this until the day before!!! Your own school, publication, film, comic strip, whatever will receive major publicity if we succeed, however — hope that this time at least that will compensate for your personal outlay.

FLYERS:

Everyone has the privilege of preparing a one-page flyer for the interest of their choice — selling a book, an idea, a film, a newsletter, etc. — which will be combined with the others in an $8^1/_2$ by 11 envelope and distributed to the participants. We want to avoid commercialism through lobby sales, but this will be a high-interest intense group we attract. If they are rewarded by the ideas they hear, they will be certain to want to hear more.

If you want to put a flyer in the pot you'll need to make 3,000 copies of it (6 reams of paper) and send it to a central collection point for assembly with everyone else's. I know B.J. has a book to sell; I do, too. Jamaal and Victor want apprenticeship opportunities and wouldn't mind some kind of part-time work, either, that teaches something. Roland has a film to attract backers for. Mary has an education journal to sell subscriptions for, so does Pat. I don't know if Dave wants to participate in this, but he's certainly welcome.

The Best of Best Regards,

John Taylor Gatto

II.

The curriculum and procedures of compulsory government schooling derive from an exhausted perspective of human potential and a social destiny bequeathed to us by Enlightenment thinkers and by a powerful synthetic philosophy known as Positivism which greatly influenced architects of American mass schooling. The same ideas — including a notion families could not be trusted to bring up their own children — had a mighty impact on business interests, too, operating as a kind of religious blueprint among society's leaders during the gestation period of compulsion schooling.

The idea there is only one right way to school and that the State must manage that way, is profoundly Positivistic, but sophisticated readers will also see that it leads them back through Hobbes and Bacon to the ancient Near East. This very old idea of a State socially engineered by experts to reach comprehensively into every corner of human life is a compelling one — but also one soundly rejected throughout European history — until waves of mass immigration provided Public Terror among established classes in the northeastern United States about 1845. New institutions sprang up quickly to deal with the menace: chief among them being state-controlled schooling. A constellation of support mechanisms which eventually included uniform testing, licensing, a radical new adoption law, Children's Courts, medical policing, State police forces and cradle-to-grave surveillance followed in the van.

Our form of schooling creates an abundance of social pathologies and contradicts the way children actually learn — sacrificing human potential to an obsession with hierarchy, order, routine, surveillance, and the creation of lifelong dependence on "expert" authority. This latter function of schooling has come to support many parasitic forms of employment in our economy. Bertrand Russell once called American schooling the most extreme social experiment in Western history, a mechanism to realize Plato's *Republic.*

Of course it has failed miserably in every measure except on its own terms. In undertaking to expose that failure in a positive way, The Odysseus Group hit on a strategy which led to Carnegie Hall on November 13, 1991 and a program of working alternatives to our form of schooling called "The Exhausted School." Although the operating budget was limited to the small savings of a public school teacher and one of his former students, the decision was made to rent glamorous Carnegie Hall because the unlikelihood of little people taking a world famous showplace to speak their mind was reckoned to provide a dramatic symbol of what is possible.

The immediate purpose was to do what no college or State Department of Education had ever done: to demonstrate a range of choices already operating outside media attention, to show wonderful alternatives, all of them much cheaper and much more effective than so-called "public" schools. A mid-range purpose was to give strong support to plans for stimulating competition in schooling by returning the economic reins to parents and communities. If Holland, Sweden, Denmark and other modern nations can pay the tuition of every child to any school he wishes, then why not here? Early American education, for the first 200 years of our history, was wonderfully hydra-headed and wonderfully effective. There were a lot of "right" ways to grow up. We wanted those privileges of choice returned.

But our long-range purpose was to revitalize grass roots democracy by showing people they could demand to be heard by the simple expedient of bypassing the official stewards of schooling: government agencies, school boards, think tanks, colleges, establishment "reform" initiatives, and the like. And so we did. What we were not prepared for was the swift and massive campaign of sabotage from existing interests, nor the silence of the press in regard to this unusual endeavor. A silence doubly curious because the host of the evening, John Taylor Gatto, was the current New York State Teacher of the Year, and had three times been named New York City Teacher of the Year. Mr. Gatto had a string of commendations from American presidents, governors, publishers and celebrities recognizing his unusual success as a front-line practitioner of an original curriculum design he calls "The Lab School." His articles critical of schooling had appeared in *The Wall Street Journal*, *The Christian Science Monitor*, and newspapers from Miami to Vancouver.

Thus, the failure to attract underwriting to advertise the show, and a general press failure to acknowledge detailed press releases as it approached was puzzling. Still, ticket sales were going well. Then a bombshell dropped. Two bus loads of attendees had been booked from the State University at New Paltz, several hours north of the City. Suddenly a call came in cancelling the group from SUNY/New Paltz. Why? "They are putting tremendous pressure on us, we don't dare come down." *Who* was exerting the pressure? "I can't tell you, I'm too ashamed," and with that, our correspondent rung off.

After that clues came thick and fast. A highly-placed official of Bank Street College had been a next-door neighbor of John Gatto's when they were growing up, but three letters asking for support for the school-choice event went unanswered from the childhood associate! A dozen profitable "school reform" initiatives originate from various professors at Columbia Teachers College, well-funded by school districts, foundations, government sources, and corporations. Not one of the school reform crowd at Columbia responded to letters, or called to inquire what was going on with "The Exhausted School." This frosty silence was repeated from Fordham University — a major player in the New York School Game, from Queens College of the City University, from City College from LIU, and elsewhere. No questions, no comments. Silence.

A personal visit to the Vanderbilt University sponsored "Educational Excellence Network" in Washington, D.C. seemed to spark interest and many questions — but the follow-up was silence. As far as its journal "Network News and Views" was concerned, Carnegie Hall didn't happen. Nor did it happen for *Teacher* magazine, for the UFT, for the AFT, for The New York City Board of Education, for the New York State Education Department, or any of the other players who make their livings from schooling exactly as it is. Change, it seemed, was to be preempted too!

Meanwhile, something even more sinister was taking place — a fact we learned to our horror two weeks before the show. In the financing of such events, fund-raisers regularly call on sources well known to be supportive of such things. In the case of "The Exhausted School," three such sources had taken the lead to contact Odysseus Group! Nothing could be more promising than that, it seemed. We were wrong. Each of our potential angels and a whole spread of others as yet untried were reached by some unknown agency and warned away from Carnegie Hall.

Who was doing this? Through some adroit detective work and drawing on favors owed, our volunteer fund-raiser disclosed her astonishing conclusion: It was the president of a prestigious foundation on Vanderbilt Avenue, she said, an institution which claimed hegemony in school reform! She confronted him, she continued, but he denied even knowing about Carnegie Hall. That was the clincher. She produced a photocopy of an information inquiry about the event written by the president himself months before to a friend of hers!

Nothing could be done, of course, but press on. Eventually 1,024 people paid their way into Carnegie Hall in spite of the media blackout, the absence of advertising, and a desperate attempt on the part of the *"reformers"* to destroy our attempt to establish a grass roots voice. An additional 800 people got in on free passes, allowing Odysseus to offer a large group of people, for the first time, a look at what the school establishment and its allies in press and government had managed to conceal from the general public — *how* schools that work actually do it. The fact that all of them "do it" on much less money than government schools need is the best explanation of the efforts to shut the evening down in the public imagination.

Finally, a word about our "method" in assembling the program. Six separate logics of schooling were unfolded that night. Superficial similarities aside, no two were really alike. Indeed, some of the principals disliked each other thoroughly and several weren't on speaking terms. Harmony obviously was beside the point.

But right *on* the point was the powerful truth that there are many fine ways to "school" children — including the way of those intrepid homeschoolers who don't school at all. Five of the six principals were ardent champions of breaking the economic monopoly government schools possess (through their exclusive use of taxing power). They say, "Give us back a share of our tax money and we will buy the best schooling for our children, public, private, parochial." But careful readers will detect that one of the speakers, a public school principal, says "No!," that doing that will "weaken" the public schools. In a different type of forum we might have asked him why a failed institution should be guaranteed its income by the police power of the State, but that would have been to contradict the terms of free discussion.

And make no mistake about it, free and open discussion is what you have been cheated of by monopoly schooling and its bully boys for too long. "The Exhausted School" program was an object lesson in what the government system has done wrong, it argued best by its own example. And so our lone dissenter — who operates a fine school program, albeit "public" — was welcome too.

One final word — six logics of schooling are treated in the following pages, *but they are far from the only sensible ways that people school.* A properly funded "Exhausted School" program could easily show *sixty* choices, brilliantly enlarging the presently stunted public imagination about what can be done. You have only six here before you because we just ran out of money, no other reason!　　　　　◆

Three Rules For This Evening's Class

by Victor Gonzalez

> **"The second rule is...no water. You can't have any water while the show is going on...If you get thirsty that's too bad — you should have thought of that before you sat down."**

Good Evening. Welcome to "The Exhausted School." Tonight we hope to teach you something about school...and something about education. They are not the same things. People who make a living from the school business would like to think that they are...but they are not. Benjamin Franklin was an educated man, but he hardly saw the inside of a school, and Thomas Jefferson never did. An education gives you the power to make your own decisions and a schooling teaches you to follow the lead of other people — not the same thing at all.

Since I've had a lot of experience with *schools*, I feel pretty comfortable warning you about your behavior while we're together. We'll get along just fine if you follow a few simple rules I have to follow myself every day.

The first rule is...don't go to the toilet without asking *my permission* ...I've arranged for the guards to lock the doors so you can't get in without a written pass...

The second rule is...no water. You can't have any water while the show is going on. If you get thirsty that's too bad — you should have thought of that before you sat down. If you're caught out of your seat going for water, I'll send for your mother...

The third rule is...I'll ring a loud BELL every forty minutes. When you hear it, drop whatever you're doing and move to another row. You have exactly three minutes to do this...don't be late. We'll take attendance in the new rows...and two latenesses equal one absence! I don't want to humiliate any of you but I will if I have to...

We'll have a multiple choice test at Intermission. Be sure to use a Number 2 pencil...bubble in your answers carefully. If you open your test booklet before I tell you to your paper will be torn to pieces in front of your eyes...

At this point I'm going to turn you over to the New York State Teacher of the Year to try to convince you that there really is a better way to learn. He's from Pittsburgh, Pennsylvania, and he was my own eighth grade teacher long, long ago...last June. He hates schooling...but he loves education. Ladies and gentlemen...my friend and my teacher ...John Taylor Gatto.   ◆

How Did We Ever Come To Believe...?

by John Taylor Gatto

> " Without children and old people mixing in daily life, a community has no future and no past, only a continuous present. "

Keep in mind as I speak that I spent 26 years in public school classrooms. My perspective is that of an insider, not an outsider. You have been warned.

We live in a time of great school crisis, and that crisis is linked to a greater social crisis in the general community. We seem to have lost our identity. Children and old people are locked away from the business of the world to a degree without precedent — nobody talks to them anymore. Without children and old people mixing in daily life, a community has no future and no past, only a continuous present.

We live in networks, not communities. Everyone I know is lonely because of that. In some strange way school is a major actor in this tragedy, just as it is a major actor in the widening gulf among races and social classes. Using school as a sorting mechanism, we appear to be on the way to creating a caste system, complete with untouchables who wander through subway trains begging, and sleep upon the streets.

I've noticed a fascinating phenomenon in my 26 years of teaching: schools and schooling are increasingly irrelevant to the great enterprises of the planet. No one believes any more that scientists are made in science classes, or politicians in civics classes, or poets in English classes. The truth is that schools don't really teach anything except how to obey orders. This is a great mystery because thousands of humane, caring people work in schools as teachers and aides, and even as administrators. But the abstract logic of the institution overwhelms their individual contributions. Although teachers *do* care, and *do* work very hard, the institution is psychopathic — by which I mean it has no conscience.

It rings a bell and the young man in the middle of writing a poem must close his notebook and move to a different cell where he memorizes that man and monkeys derive from a common ancestor, or that a man named Columbus discovered America even though millions of people were already here.

The idea that schooling and education are the same thing was never a convincing one, but in our lifetimes, yours and mine, it has become an exhausted one.

How did we ever come to believe that the State should tell our children what to think?

To escape the trap we are in will require acts of courage and imagination: the first an act of political resolve —to deconstruct the kind of schooling we have and return it to real people and real communities from abstract government hands; the second, to create a vision of *what* can be done and how to do it. My own job tonight will be to question the legitimacy of the school monopoly. In the hours we are together, you'll hear six separate logics of schooling, as different from each other as they are from the logic of government factory schools where I spend my own working life.

If you had a choice where to send your own kid you might well choose one of these six ideas, yet still be grateful you *knew* about the other five, even if they were not the right way for you. But the secret strength in this simple program design is that they do *not* represent all the worthwhile kinds of schooling. Many more exist concealed from view by the government monopoly and its press agents. These are unique, one-of-a-kind places you'll hear from tonight — their existence proving there is no "one right way" to grow up.

How on earth did we ever accept the idea a government had the right to tell us where to go to school? How did we ever come to believe the State should tell our children what to think?

2.

Our form of compulsion schooling is an invention of the State of Massachusetts, 140 years ago. It was resisted, sometimes with guns, by an estimated 80 percent of the Massachusetts population. A senator's office contended not too long ago that prior to compulsory government schooling the literacy rate in Massachusetts was 98 percent, but after it the figure never again reached above 91 percent.

I don't think we'll get rid of schools anytime soon, certainly not in my lifetime, but if we're going to change what has become a disaster we need to recognize that ignorance is inherent in the design of the thing. It is not the fault of bad teachers, or of too little money spent. Structurally, schools fly in the face of how children learn.

Take reading. People learn to read naturally and easily somewhere between the ages of 5 and 12, some earlier, some later. Late readers are indistinguishable from early readers in a very short time. But the natural course of things can be violently altered by rewarding early readers — and by pronouncing later readers "in need of remediation." The lie is then compounded by supplying the deficient with "special" treatment, including assignment to a separate junk category called "special education." You cannot "teach" children to read any more than you can "teach" them to walk and talk. Under the right conditions they teach themselves with great facility.

But you *can* teach children to *hate* reading, to do it poorly, and to hate themselves for not measuring up to the false premises of institutional reading practice — premises which provide the foundation for our multi-billion dollar reading industry. The reading racket, in particular, has marked the burgeoning home school movement for legal sanctions because the presence of nearly a million children who've taught themselves to read, soundly and happily, creates a clear and present danger to the "whole word" crowd and to the "phonics" crowd alike. Bad for business.

◆

Schools as we know them haven't been around very long. They don't have deep roots. That's one thing in our favor as we think about uprooting them. Schools as we have them were designed at the time of the American Civil War to be instruments for the scientific management of a mass population, the cheap labor immigration was providing to factory and farm. Schools are intended to produce through the application of formulae, formulaic human beings whose behavior can be predicted and controlled.

To a very great extent schools succeed in doing this. But in a nation increasingly disintegrated and demoralized, in a national order where the only successful people are independent, self-reliant, confident, and individualistic, the products of schooling are irrelevant. Well-schooled people are irrelevant. They can sell film and razor blades, push paper and talk on telephones, make deals or sit mindlessly before a flickering computer terminal, but they hate to be alone with themselves. As human beings they are useless.

I spoke in southern Illinois last week. During my talk a young man about 25 years old stood up in the back of the room and said in a tormented voice, "I'm 25 years old and have two college degrees. I don't know how to do *anything*. I don't know how to do anything at all. If the fan belt of my car broke in a snowstorm out in the country I'd freeze to death reciting the goddamn Pythagorean theorem."

Much daily misery around us is caused by the fact our schools force children to grow up absurd. Any reform in schooling must deal with its absurdities: it is absurd and anti-life to be part of a system that compels you to sit in confinement with people exactly the same age and social class. That system effectively cuts you off from information you need to be sane, and cuts you off from your own past and future. It seals you into a continuous present much the same way television does. It is absurd and anti-life to be part of a system compelling you to listen to a stranger read poetry when you ache to learn to construct buildings; it is absurd and anti-life to sit with a stranger discussing the construction of buildings when the rush of language inside you makes you want to write a poem.

It is absurd and anti-life to move from cell to cell at the sound of a buzzer, every day of your natural youth, in an institution that allows you no private time or space.

What parent would allow such a horror to be inflicted if their own schooling had left them with the power to understand? "What about `basics'?" you say. If you are willing to face the truth you would see that only talking is basic to the society we've made. We are a land of talkers now. We pay talkers most and admire talkers most — and so our children talk constantly, following public models of television, radio, and school teachers. It is very difficult to get children to take "basics" seriously these days — especially in the social environment of schools — because they really *aren't* basic to the world we've forced on the children. None of us stays silent long enough to figure out what the new basics really are.

3.

wo institutions control our children's lives — television and schooling, probably in that order. Both reduce the real world to a never-ending, nonstop abstraction. For most of history until recently, the time of a child would be occupied in real work, real charity, real adventures, real apprenticeships, and the realistic search for mentors who might teach what you really needed to learn. What that is, is of course, different for each of us.

A great deal of time was spent in community pursuits, practicing affection, negotiating, and studying every level of the society around you firsthand. Also in learning how to make a home, a living, and dozens of other tasks necessary to become a whole man or woman. *There was a continuity and a comprehensiveness to life.* It was not fragmented into subjects and specialties to provide work for professionals, nor was it arranged into sequences that made no sense. The kind of education history reveals was administered most often by people you *knew* — not by total strangers arranged into a priesthood called "teachers."

◆

In the new world order that was arranged for us after the Civil War the calculus was changed. Scientific Positivism, as it used to be called, wanted the calculus changed and Horace Mann and Frederick Taylor were nothing if they were not religiously Positivist. Today the tabulation of hours in a young life reads like this: My children watch television 55 hours a week according to recent reports, and they sleep 56. That leaves them 57 hours in which to grow up strong and competent and whole. But my children attend school 30 hours more, spend 8 hours preparing for school, and in goings and comings, and an additional 7 hours a week in something called "home"-work — although this is really more schoolwork except in "Newspeak." After those 45 school hours are removed a total of 12 hours remain each week from which to fashion a private person — one that can like, trust, and live with itself. Twelve hours. But my kids must eat, too, and that takes some time. Not much, because they've lost the tradition of family dining — how they learn to eat in school is best called "feeding" — but if we allot just 3 hours a week to evening feedings, we arrive at a net total of private time for each child of 9 hours.

It's not enough. It's not enough, is it? The richer the kid the less TV he watches, of course, but the rich kid's time is just as narrowly proscribed by his inevitable assignments to private lessons from more hired strangers, seldom in areas of his own actual choice.

This demented schedule is an efficient way to create dependent human beings, needy people unable to fill their own hours, unable to initiate lines of meaning to give substance and pleasure to their existence. It is a national disease, this dependency and aimlessness, and schooling and television and busy work — the total Chautauqua package — has a lot to do with it.

Think of the things killing us as a nation: narcotic drugs, brainless competition, dishonesty, greed, recreational sex, the pornography of violence, gambling, alcohol, and the worst pornography of all — lives devoted to buying things, accumulation as a philosophy — all of these are addictions of dependent personalities. That is what our brand of schooling must inevitably produce. A large fraction of our total economy has grown up around providing service and counseling to inadequate people — and inadequate people are the main product of government compulsion schools.

4.

I want to tell you what the effect is on children of taking the time they need to grow up and forcing them to spend it on abstractions. No reform that brainlessly defines our national problem as reading, writing, and arithmetic will be anything more than a coward's evasion of the nightmare we've inflicted on our children.

The children I teach are indifferent to the adult world. This defies the experience of thousands of years. Nobody wants to grow up these days because assuming responsibility takes practice, but schooltime precludes practice.

The children I teach have almost no curiosity. What curiosity they do have is transitory, they cannot even concentrate long on jobs they assign themselves. Can you see a possible connection between bells ringing again and again to change classes and this phenomenon of evanescent attention? When everything you do is interrupted before it's finished, why should you care about anything?

The children I teach have a poor sense of the future, of how tomorrow is linked to today. The exact moment they are in is the boundary of their consciousness. That was the dream of a 19th century Frenchman named Auguste Comte, and before he died in the insane asylum at Charenton his ideas had a profound impact on Horace Mann and the American schoolroom, and on Frederic Taylor and the American workplace.

The children I teach have no sense of the past and how it predestinated the present, how it limits their choices, how it shapes their lives and values. A long line of Western thinkers, all of them childless men like Comte, have understood that breaking a child's ties with the past cracks him away from his own family. And separating parents and children has been the goal of childless male philosophers since Plato wrote about its value in *The Republic*. Without strong family ties, he said, children are easier subjects for central planning. Augustine knew that, and Erasmus, and Bacon, and Descartes, and Hobbes, and Rousseau — and all the other childless men who helped to architect the government schooling we have today.

The children I teach are cruel to each other; they lack compassion for misfortune, they laugh at weakness, they have contempt for people whose need for help shows too plainly.

The children I teach are uneasy with intimacy, solitude, or unguarded speech. They cannot deal with genuine intimacy because of a lifelong habit of preserving a secret inner self beneath their public school personalities, personalities which must remain open at all times, as a prostitute's body is open to the constant inspection and ranking of strangers. Our children's public personalities are kept constantly under surveillance by authorities in an orgy of voyeurism. The outer persona of the children I teach is fabricated from artificial bits and pieces of behavior borrowed from television, or acquired by studying the preferences of schoolteachers. The real self is too small and vulnerable to bear longtime exposure, because it has had no privacy in which to develop strength and integrity. Since exposure is required in intimate relationships, these must be avoided. My children are not who they pretend to be. Most of them aren't anybody at all, thanks to school. It's frightening.

The children I teach are strikingly materialistic, following the lead of schoolteachers who materialistically "grade" everything, and television mentors who offer everything in the world for sale.

The children I teach are dependent, passive, timid in the presence of new challenges. This timidity is often masked by surface bravado, by the exuberance of youth, by anger or aggressiveness, but underneath the bluster is emptiness, mirroring the great vacuum, the black hole of government schooling which draws in vast energies, but emits little.

I could name other conditions school reform must tackle, but by now you will have grasped my thesis. Schools and television *cause* these pathologies. It's a simple matter of arithmetic. Between schooling and television all the time children have to become adults is eaten up. That is what has destroyed the American family; it is no longer a factor in the education of its own young, it no longer has access to its own children.

5.

*T*onight's program is one of choices, choices for parents, choices for young people, choices for communities. Where did we ever get the crazy idea that government had the right to tell us how our own kids should grow up?

Where did we ever get the grotesque idea that the State has a right to educate our kids? Where did we ever get the notion there is only one right way to grow up instead of hundreds? How did we lose our way and come to believe that human value and human quality can be reduced to numbers derived from paper/pencil tests? ◆

How To Get An Education At Home

by Pat Farenga

" My friend, the late John Holt, wrote about how people learn... He spent the better part of his life demonstrating that we can trust children to learn all the time. "

There is a revolution going on in education, but it is not happening in schools. It is happening in the homes of American families in every state. It is happening every time a family decides to help its children learn at home instead of sending them to school. Fourteen years ago there were roughly 10,000 children being homeschooled; now there are upwards of 600,000 children learning at home. If you and your children are not pleased with your schools and you are tired of waiting for them to change, then you can do something now and join the growing ranks of people who homeschool.

It is impossible to generalize about the "typical" homeschooling family any more than you can about the "typical" family whose children attend schools. Homeschoolers include traditional, middle-class two parent households, single parents, low-income families, families with parents or children who have physical disabilities, and two-income families. Some homeschool solely for religious reasons; some homeschool solely for pedagogical reasons. Many homeschool for mixtures of both reasons, and many others homeschool simply because they enjoy being with their children and watching them learn. Some homeschoolers live in rural communes; others live in midtown Manhattan. Some homeschooling parents have only high school diplomas, others have doctorates. It is not necessary to have a teaching certificate to homeschool effectively. None of these examples are conjectural; families homeschooling under these and other conditions have been writing to us at *Growing Without Schooling* with their stories for over fourteen years. All sorts of people homeschool, and you can too.

You might think that homeschooled children are limited by their parents' expertise, experience, and knowledge. If we view teaching as the filling up of an empty bottle with the teacher's knowledge then this concern makes sense. With only one or two people pouring into the child's "bottle" it makes sense that the child will only learn what they pour in. However, homeschooling allows you to depart from the "bottle" model of school learning and follow a different concept of how children learn.

My friend, the late John Holt, wrote about how people learn throughout his ten books about education. He spent the better part of his life demonstrating that we can trust children to learn all the time. John observed that for children under school age, living and learning are interconnected, but once they enter school, the two are separated. Learning is supposed to take place in special buildings called schools, and living takes place outside of school. But from the moment children are born they learn from everything they have access to, not just from special teachers and places. Children learn to walk and talk with little or no formal teaching from us parents. Several studies have noted that homeschooled children consistently test at or above grade level when compared to their schooled age-mates, *regardless* of the degrees attained or teacher certification of their parents. Washington, Alaska, and Alabama are three states that have studied and reported this. This proves not only that we can trust our children to learn, but that we can trust ourselves to be effective teachers for our children.

"But I'm not good at math," you may be thinking. "How could I be a good homeschooling parent?" First, homeschoolers use a wide variety of resources and learning materials. Some feel more comfortable beginning with a fairly traditional curriculum, and many different ones are readily available. Other families follow a less conventional approach, learning according to their own timetables and taking advantage of individual learning. Many parents find homeschooling greatly stimulates their own thinking and creativity and provides them with new learning opportunities.

Homeschoolers also think very hard about friends, relations, neighbors, and co-workers who have expertise in areas their children want to explore. We hear many stories about how non-family members offer considerable help with a child's home education. One child decided she wanted to learn more math than her mother was familiar with. Her mother found a math tutor for her. Another story is about how a boy learned a great deal about computer programming from adults he met at his church and through Scouts. Amber Clifford, a sixteen-year-old homeschooler from Missouri, wrote to us about her interest in archaeology, something her parents know nothing about. "I was able to do the reading and studying on my own, but my parents helped me find the resource people that I needed and took me to the places that I needed to see. We're in a town with a university, so when I was interested in fossils, my mother called the geology department and got the professor to talk to me. I didn't know how to go about finding someone, and she did, so this is where she was really helpful to me."

Some of you may feel that the children I am describing are special, that homeschoolers are taking the best and most motivated children out of school and leaving school with the dregs. The fact is that many of the children now flourishing in homeschools *were not* flourishing in school. Some parents began homeschooling children who had been labeled "learning disabled" in school, and they watched their children lose their LD behavior. Other homeschoolers have children for whom school was not challenging enough, and they teach them at home using materials and experiences that match their needs. Some homeschooled children are late readers, not learning to read until they are ten or so. Grant Colfax, a homeschooled child who graduated from Harvard and is now in medical school, didn't learn to read until he was nine. Woodrow Wilson, who was homeschooled, learned to read when he was eleven. Children like Colfax and Wilson develop other talents and skills while they are young, and when they do learn to read they do so without special difficulty. In school these late readers would be immediately segregated and treated for these academic deficiencies, and they would be held back from other learning opportunities until they could read at their grade level. It is simply not true that all homeschoolers would be winners in school anyway.

Despite the diversity of methods and reasons for homeschooling, there is one thing each and every homeschooler has in common: they are all asked, "How will your children be socialized if they don't go to school?"

Homeschooling allows children to participate and learn in the real world. It allows them to mix with much younger and much older people, take courses as they want or need them, and apprentice with people they can learn from in the community. Homeschoolers play with their friends in their neighborhood and make friends with other homeschoolers. A young homeschooler in Pennsylvania wrote to us about her experience volunteering at a home for disabled kids; a family from California wrote to us about their son's work in a soup kitchen. Many families write to us about how their children participate in community theater, give music lessons to younger children in their neighborhood, or share hobbies with fellow enthusiasts of all ages. Homeschoolers have apprenticed at historical societies, veterinarian's offices, architecture firms, nature centers, and many other places. Serena Gingold, a homeschooled youngster from California, wrote to us about her involvement in local politics: "I've written letters to the editor about my opinions. You really learn a lot about opinions when you publicly voice your own. I've also been publicly criticized, and my county fair projects were censored because they were `too political' (actually because I was too political for a kid). One letter in the paper criticized me for being a kid and having opinions! People always say I should go to school so I can learn about the real world, but I'm *living* in the real world!"

Certainly group experiences *are* a big part of education, and homeschoolers have plenty of them. Homeschoolers write to us about how they form or join writing clubs, book discussion groups, and local homeschooling support groups. Homeschoolers also take part in school sports teams and music groups, as well as the many public and private group activities our communities provide. For example, Kristin Williams of Michigan recently wrote to our magazine, *Growing Without Schooling,* about how they meet many different types of people. "We're a black family living in a racially and economically mixed neighborhood," she writes. "…We don't really go out looking for people who are different from ourselves. Many come through the family: a cousin has an Arab-American girlfriend, another had a Japanese mother-in-law, another is married to an Afro-Canadian, one to a Polish-American, still another to a Jamaican and one to a Nigerian." She writes how through church, 4-H club, and neighbors they have encountered and enjoyed many different types of people. At home they play tapes of foreign music, listen to overseas shortwave radio broadcasts, cook ethnic foods, and go to international fairs and multi-cultural worship services.

Homeschoolers can and do experience other people and cultures without going to school.

The flipside of socialization is solitary reflection. Homeschooling allows children to have some time alone, time to pursue their own thoughts and interests. Children, like adults, need time to be alone to think, to muse, to read freely, to daydream, to be creative, to form a self independent of the barrage of mass culture.

A British man once remarked to me how amazing it was to him that Americans expect schools to socialize their children. "I always thought the social graces were taught at home," he said. This observation is supported by a recent study in the *Journal of Personality and Social Psychology*. This study tracked how childhood experiences — in and out of school — affected adult development over a 36-year period. The study concluded that the only factor that showed a significant effect by itself on children's social maturity and their later social accomplishment as adults was "parental warmth and affection."

You may find that you teach your children at home for just a semester, for a year, or forever. The choice is yours, not school's. The entry or reentry of homeschooled children into the classroom appears to be no different than for those who transfer into a school from another district.

Homeschooling works because *schooling is not the same thing as education*. School is not the only place to learn, to grow up. Universities and colleges recognize this fact whenever they admit homeschoolers who have never attended school. Homeschoolers who never attended, or rarely attended, any schools are currently students at Harvard, Boston University, Rice University, and the Curtis Institute of Music, to name a few. In addition, homeschoolers who decide *not* to go to college are finding adult work without special difficulty. Some of the homeschoolers I know who fall into this category are currently employed in the fields of computers, ballet, theater, movies, aviation, construction, and overseas missionary work.

Consider these famous people who were homeschooled for some or all of their school years: Authors William Blake, Charles Dickens, Pearl Buck, Agatha Christie and Margaret Atwood; social and political figures Benjamin Franklin, Woodrow Wilson, Winston Churchill, Samuel Gompers, Charles Lindberg, Florence Nightingale; artists Andrew Wyeth, Yehudi Menuhin, Sean O'Casey, Charlie Chaplin, Claude Monet, and Noel Coward; inventors Thomas Edison and the Wright brothers. One of the world's richest men, the man for whom this hall is named, Andrew Carnegie, was homeschooled until he was nine. He was coaxed into attending school after that, but by the age of thirteen

Carnegie left school and never went back. School attendance is not the only way to become a successful, sociable adult.

Vita Wallace, a homeschooler from Pennsylvania, wrote these words when she turned sixteen and officially graduated from home-schooling: "The most important thing I think I have gained through my education is that I know what I love to do. I think if I had gone to school I wouldn't have had time to find out. I know it's awfully confusing for people when, after graduating from thirteen years of schooling, they still don't know... I've been able to make friends with all kinds of different people — people younger, the same age, and older than I am; my teachers, colleagues and students; my neighbors young and old; my parents' friends, my brother's friends and teachers; and most important, my brother. He's been my best friend all along, and I am so glad we didn't go to school if only for the one reason that we might not have been able to be such bosom buddies otherwise..."

Homeschooling is not a panacea to all our educational problems, but it *is* part of the answer. It is a proven option for any of you who wish to try it. ◆

School For A Post-Industrial Society

by Dan Greenberg

"If you come to Sudbury Valley, the first impression you get is that of a regular school in recess."

Three hundred years ago, if somebody had ventured the opinion it is possible to create a country in which people from all walks of life, all persuasions, nationalities, and backgrounds could live together in freedom, peace, and harmony, could live happy lives, could realize their personal dreams — a country in which people showed each other mutual respect, in which people treated each other with complete equality, and in which all decisions were made by the mutual consent of the governed, people would have considered that person a crazy utopian and would have brought all the experience of human history from the dawn of time as witness to the impossibility of such a dream. They would have said, "People just don't live that way. It doesn't work. It can't happen."

Happily for us sitting here today, two centuries ago our founding fathers did not treat that dream as utopian and instead found a way to make it possible to put it into practice. They did something unique in the history of the human race. They had before them the task of creating a new country, a new form of government. And they set about this task not by revising existing forms of government, not by starting from the models that they had around them and tinkering with them and adding a little here and a little there, but by sitting together and spending a tremendous amount of time and thought on "zero-base planning," on creating a government from scratch, starting from no assumptions other than those that they were willing to make explicit at the moment. We have records of their deliberations, and many writings that reveal what they thought and how they came to their conclusions. They proceeded by examining the condition of the human race, the nature of the human animal, and the social and cultural conditions of the world into which the country they were founding was going to be born.

The founders of Sudbury Valley School, beginning in 1965, did much the same thing when it came to education. We too were dissatisfied — dissatisfied with the models of schools that we had available to us at the time, and we had a deep conviction that there was more at stake than just the proper curriculum or the right pedagogical methodology or the right mix of social and emotional and psychological factors that had to be applied to the educational scene. We were convinced that the time had come for complete re-examination of what it is that a school had to be about if it were to serve as an appropriate agent of society in this country in the late 20th century and beyond the year 2000. So we spent several years working on this, trying to gain an understanding of what school is for and how the goals of schools can best be realized.

Now, it's pretty much generally agreed that there are two major roles that a school fills. One is to provide an environment in which children can grow to maturity, from a state of formativeness and dependence to a state of independence as adults who have found their unique way of personal expression in life. The second goal is social rather than individual. The school has to be the environment in which the culture prepares itself for its continuation from generation to generation. This is a goal that a community requires of its educational system if it wants its way of life to survive.

There is no guarantee that the social goal and the individual goal will mesh. In an authoritarian society, for example, where the lives of every single individual are controlled by some central authority, the social goal promulgating the authoritarian system is in clear conflict with any primacy given to the individual goals of the people in that society. One of the functions of a school in an authoritarian society must

44

therefore be to subject the individual to severe restraints in order to force that individual to meet the needs of society as a whole. The educational systems of highly authoritarian regimes play down individual variation and individual freedom and effectively try to eliminate them.

On the other hand, in anarchistic educational systems, the individual is focused on, almost entirely to the exclusion of society. The individual is elevated above all else and modes of social interaction and cultural survival are given very little attention.

When we started thinking about Sudbury Valley School, we had no way of knowing whether there would be any way of harmonizing individual needs and social needs in the United States today. We started by examining the social side because it was clear to us that no school could possibly survive if it didn't meet the needs of modern American society. It might survive as a fringe school for some few discontented people who perhaps wanted a different way of life in this country. But as an institution that was meaningful to the mainstream of American society, there was no hope for it to survive unless it could tie into the deep needs of American culture in this era. So we set about asking ourselves, "What is it really that the society wants today in order to flourish?"

The key to the answer to this question was the realization that the United States is fundamentally a free market economy in which personal freedom is maximized on a social level. Ours is a society which, as a community, extols personal freedoms for its individual members and has social ways of guaranteeing these freedoms through the grant of rights and redress to individuals. In addition, the United States, in 1965, was clearly entering an economic era which was a novelty on the world scene — namely, the post-industrial economic era, which was beginning to be recognized as a reality. Today, of course, the image of a post-industrial society is commonplace. The key concept which differentiates a post-industrial economy from an industrial economy is the realization that in a post-industrial society, in principle, every task that can be defined by a set routine can be taken out of human hands and put into the hands of some sort of information processing machine. The main difference between an industrial and a post-industrial society lies not in the presence or absence of produced goods, but in the means by which those goods are produced. In an industrial society it is essential to have a virtual ARMY of human beings who are fit somehow into the mechanism of the overall industrial machine, who play an integrated role in the production process as parts of the machine.

The strength of the industrial society was that by using machines, it could magnify many, many thousandfold the ability of the society to produce material benefits for its members. But the machines couldn't do this alone. The machines were not sophisticated enough to carry out this process unaided. In order to make it happen what was needed was human intervention and human help. Human and machine became as one, something that probably has never been better illustrated than in the great classic film *Modern Times* that Charlie Chaplin produced over fifty years ago.

The deal that was made by various societies, one after the other, when they chose to enter the industrial era was to agree to forfeit much of their humanity, much of their freedom as individuals, in order to benefit as a society from the wealth and prosperity that the industrial era promised. This isn't an altogether ridiculous deal by any means. It's perfectly understandable that human societies that for thousands of years had accepted as inevitable the grinding poverty and deprivation and misery of the overwhelming majority of people — it's not surprising that such societies, when faced with the promise that miraculously and with incredible suddenness virtually the entire population could raise its standard of living and survive in a relatively comfortable manner, chose, one after another, to sacrifice willingly some of their personal freedoms, many of which were illusory anyway, to achieve that goal.

The post-industrial era is of a different nature, however. The post-industrial era asks no sacrifice of the material benefits that the industrial era provided. On the contrary, the development of sophisticated, computer-driven machines and information processing systems has promised an even greater degree of national wealth and diversity. But the demands on the individual are now completely different. In the post-industrial society there is essentially no place for human beings who are not able to function independently. There is no room for people trained to be cogs in a machine. Such people have been displaced permanently from the economic system. The needs of a post-industrial society, regardless of the governmental structure, are for people who can be independent, entrepreneurial producers of economic benefits. People have to take initiative to think for themselves, to create for themselves, to become productive for themselves. In a post-industrial society, there is no longer a mass of predetermined slots into which to fit people. The economic demands of post-industrial America are something that you hear from personnel directors in every industry and company today, small or large. The demands are for creative people with initiative, self-starters, people who know how to take responsibility, exercise judgment, make decisions for themselves.

This meant to us that a school in post-industrial America, in order to serve the culture, has to have the following features: It has to allow for a tremendous amount of diversity. It has to allow for people to become, on their own, self-starters, initiators, entrepreneurs. And, at the same time, it has to allow children to grow up completely at home with the cultural values of our country, especially such essential values as tolerance, mutual respect, and self-government.

We then looked at the requirements for individual realization. These too had undergone a rather interesting change of perspective through the work of psychologists and developmental theorists. The commonly accepted model of the human had been that of a *tabula rasa*, a clean slate, born as infants with basically nothing in their heads and therefore growing up to be what other people have written on that slate. That's a model that put a tremendous responsibility on the people around the child who write on that child's slate. In a sense, that model was the utter negation of the individual as an independent being, and the subjugation of the individual will to the influences of those around it who impose their wills and their intellects on it from infancy onwards.

But Aristotle, 2,000 years ago, and developmental psychologists in recent times, developed other models that seemed to us, when we were creating Sudbury Valley School, to be much more realistic and much more in line with what we saw to be the nature of the human species. These people considered children from birth as being *naturally curious*, as being active participants in the learning process — not born with blank minds but, on the contrary, born with information processing systems in their brains which *require* of them, *demand* of them, by nature, to reach out, to explore, to seek to understand the world and make sense of it, using their sensory interactions and their agile brains to build pictures of reality — world views — in their minds that enable them to function in the world. In our view there was no such thing as a passive child. Every child is active. Every child we had ever seen, certainly in early infancy, was devoured with curiosity, was energetic, was able to overcome almost every barrier, was courageous, persistent, and constantly seeking to meet every challenge that came their way. And these are traits that we saw continuing year after year in children as long as it wasn't forced out of them by some crunching outside intervention.

So it seemed clear to us that the ideal environment for children to attain the full realization of their inherent intellectual, emotional, and spiritual potentials had to be one which, subject only to constraints imposed by safety, is totally open for exploration, free of restraints, free of external impositions; a place where each individual child would be granted the freedom to reach out everywhere and anywhere they

wished so that they could follow through on all of their curious prob-
ing. This realization came upon us *like a thunderclap* because we saw
such a beautiful fit between the needs of society today and the needs of
the individual. Both society and the individual in modern post-industrial America require that schools be an environment in which children
are FREE, and in which children can LEARN HOW TO USE FREE-
DOM, how to be self-governing, how to live together as free people in
peace and harmony and mutual respect. Not an environment in which
one group dominated, or exercised power over another. Not an environment in which children were put into any sort of externally imposed
track, or forced to think about prescribed subjects. But an environment
in which children and adults alike work together to guarantee free
accessibility to the world, to the greatest extent possible, for each and
every child. And that, in effect, is what Sudbury Valley school is about.

If you come to Sudbury Valley, the first impression you get is that of
a regular school in recess. You notice children, outdoors and indoors,
freely going on and off campus, freely walking about, moving from
room to room, changing from group to group, talking, interacting, reading, playing. So much playing! More than anything else, the children at
Sudbury Valley School, of all ages, play. The better they are at playing,
the better they are at fashioning new models with which to understand
the world. Play is the greatest teacher of all. Every innovative adult
who has ever written about the creative process has talked about the
extent to which he or she *played* with new ideas, moving freely in and
out of new, original conceptions of the world without being hampered
by preconceived notions of reality. The children at Sudbury Valley
know how to play. They know how to take their play seriously. They
know how to play with intensity and with focus.

Sudbury Valley is a community governed by itself. Every child in
Sudbury Valley has a vote in every matter that pertains to the school.
The school is governed by a School Meeting in which four-year-olds
have the same vote as adults. *Every decision* in the school is made by
that School Meeting. The budget, the hiring and firing of staff, the letting of contracts. In the Sudbury Valley community, no adult wields any
particular power over any child, nor does any child wield power over
any other child. All decisions are made in the School Meeting or dele-
gated by the School Meeting to people elected on a temporary basis to
fill a particular need. Our community is a model of democratic governance, much like the New England communities that we serve.

The children at Sudbury Valley, from age four and up, by being free,
learn how to function as free people in a free society. They learn how to

find their own pursuits. They learn how to occupy themselves. They learn how to create their own environments. They learn how to respect each other. They learn how to cooperate. They learn how to use the School Meeting to legislate community rules, and to forge compromises when there are mutually exclusive demands made on property, or on places, or on activities. They learn how to meet challenges. They learn how to overcome failure since there is nobody there to shield them from failure. They learn how to try something and relish success, and they learn how to try something and fail at it — and try again. All of this takes place in an environment in which there is absolutely NO outside intervention of curriculum, of guidance, of grading, of testing, of evaluation, of segregation by age, or of the imposition of arbitrary outside authority.

The school has now been running for 24 years. It has in it children of all ages. We have 125 students now and we have an incredible record of fiscal success as well as educational success. When we first started, people looking in from the outside said that if children have a real say in financial matters, their inexperience will lead them to squander the resources of the school in a profligate manner. They'll buy candy. They'll waste their money on trivialities. The facts speak otherwise. The ability of children to govern themselves is in no way less impressive than that of adults. Our school has never received one cent of government subsidy, endowment, foundation money, or any other outside funds. It is totally tuition-based. The tuition in 1968 was on a par with the public school expenditures in the schools around us — $900 per pupil. Today, 24 years later, at a time when educational costs have soared in other schools, and when all we hear is that not enough money is being spent on education, Sudbury Valley School costs about $3000 per pupil, less than half the per pupil costs of the local public schools. And that's the whole cost, including capital expenses and including all the other hidden costs that other schools write on different sets of books. The tremendous efficiency of our fiscal operation is due entirely to the manner in which decisions are made by the entire school community, and due to the extraordinarily modest expenditures required by students who are eagerly and intensely pursuing their passionate interests.

Educationally, the Sudbury Valley School has had a remarkable record. The students are bright-eyed, intelligent, articulate, and are equally comfortable conversing about ideas, climbing trees, hanging out with children ten years older or ten years younger — even with adults. They have mastered pursuits as varied as calculus, photography, french horn, skateboarding, pottery, poetry, bookkeeping, pathology, backwoods survival, leatherworking, carpentry — the list is almost as long as the number of people who have been enrolled. Despite the fact that when we started people said that our students who wanted to go on to college would never be admitted because they had no grades, no transcripts, no school recommendations, our record has been an unbroken one. We have a 100 percent rate of acceptance into colleges, trade schools, art schools and the like for every single student who has ever wanted to continue their formal education. Our students present themselves to college Admissions Officers as people who are self-contained, who know why they want to go on with their studies, who understand who they are, and who have figured out how they want to carry on with their lives. The Sudbury Valley graduate has a degree of self-knowledge, self-esteem and an awareness of his or her own strengths that is unexcelled in schools today for people of comparable age.

We feel that Sudbury Valley is a superb model of an educational environment for post-industrial America. The joy, happiness, pleasantness, friendliness, and warmth that extend to anyone who is part of the school community is palpable. Trust, too, is everywhere, and everywhere to be seen. Belongings lie unguarded, doors unlocked, equipment unprotected and available to all. We have open admissions — everyone can attend. And by walking across the threshold, become, in an instant, part of the warmth and trust that is the school.

Sudbury Valley School is a true democratic republic of children and adults working together. Does it sound utopian? It may, but no less utopian than the United States of America sounded when people first heard about it in the rest of the world. Our school, we feel, is indeed a utopia that is as real as the country of which it is a part.

Thank you.   ◆

In The Belly
Of The Dragon

by Kathleen Young

" And [the State school inspectors] said, 'The problem is you seem to like the children.' I'm not kidding, that's what they said. "

When you're going to give a speech in our circles, you want to quote somebody. The most quotable act in town is John Gatto so I had a hard time tonight figuring out how I was going to start because you've got the man himself here.

So I was pondering this and I thought I'd come up with a bit of a dragon — we always like to talk about dragons —you may not believe in them but I do. I have a feeling that all of us have arrived in the belly of the dragon. That we have, somehow, brought ourselves tonight to hear the ideals we all have (to give us courage). And I was working on this, and I was sitting at my desk, and I had a letter that I had opened. It was from France and it said, "Dear Director," or whatever it is that the book from French to English tells you to say when you're writing a letter to America, and it said: "We have heard about your school, and we have heard about the dream of Karl Ege, and we want the dream to come true in our little village in France."

And this I found most astonishing and most frightening. Because in a certain sense Karl Ege's dream has taken us to where we are — and as I just said, I think we're in the belly of the dragon — and I wondered how to answer the man.

Karl Ege was an educator. He was working here in New York City in the Rudolf Steiner school on East 79th Street. He and his colleagues thought that students in the city needed a country experience. He felt that the students needed the farm and the life on the land. He and his friends began to look for a farm. And they looked and they looked, apparently they looked at many sites, and they found a farm in Columbia County upstate, about two hours' drive, and they purchased this farm.

Now, if you go to this farm you will find a thriving, bio-dynamic place. The cows are well, the chickens are well, the pigs are well, the farmers are well, the apprentices are well... The farmers have succeeded. They make yoghurt; they have a bakery. They make quark cheese — which you can only get in Switzerland and Hawthorne Valley Farm.

Very soon after, the school started across the street from the farm. And the little school has grown to 300 students, a full nursery through 12th grade program. The dream of Karl Ege was to combine the work on the land with the work of education, and to "warm it up" — to supplement it, to make it *live* through work with artists and artisans in the community.

And so a painting school was started. And there's a little printing endeavor. There are many efforts to bring about an answer to this incredible artistic need we have. Farmers have it. Teachers have it. Students have it. Parents have it.

And there is this hope that one could integrate all these dreams together, to make *one* that would live.

In addition, we have this little house where children can come from all over, and they can stay for a week at a time in the visiting student's program. The students that visit love to get up and gather the milk and the eggs at 4 and 5 in the morning. Perhaps they study some geology, perhaps they study some botany, or perhaps they go cross-country skiing — but all have this life on the land which was part of the dream.

We have been there 18 years, and we have felt good *and* bad about what we do. Hawthorne Valley is a Waldorf School, and Waldorf schools have a whole theory about the developing child.

One day we had two or three visitors from the New York State Education Department, and we welcomed them. They were lovely people, well-dressed and articulate, very warm and interested in what we do. And these visitors were spread out in the school; they stayed for the day. And they said to us they were looking for a developmental approach to education in New York State.

That we have. So we put them in various places, and we held our breath while they went around through the day. We tried to guide them into our school life.

If they went to the kindergarten they would have seen children playing. They would have seen children baking bread or making soup. They make the most remarkable soup. It's made with a pot of water and anything any child brings in that day. I have never understood how they make such delicious soup that way! But their mothers send in either what's very fresh or what's very unfresh, whichever the case may be, and they chop it and scrape it, and they put it in the pot — and someone comes along and adds *something*, because it's a *wonderful* soup.

And the kids learn to paint — they have watercolor classes — and they do various things. But they don't learn to read, they don't have computer classes, and we hope to God they don't watch television. These children are guided through the day in play and in love and in the most beautiful surroundings we can create. They learn French. They learn German in our school. Both through song and poetry. Children are happy in our school.

If our visitor went to grades one through eight, they would have had eight *different* kinds of experiences. In our school the teacher carries a class through eight years. In our way, whatever happens between the students and the teacher has a strong element of a *bond* to it. So if I'm the teacher in the fourth grade and I've had the children for four years, I can say, "Remember when?" and "Remember when?" and, together, that *moment* is discipline enough. Both of us remember what happened then, and we can go on from there.

The teacher who carries the class, grades one through eight, has the task of changing himself or herself every day — because he must meet a growing human being. And if you *don't* change, you're the one who gets out. The children tell you instantly if you haven't understood. And you know that there's nothing wrong with *them*, there's something wrong with *you*.

You can figure it out. You go home and cry a little bit and you figure it out. And the next day there's something else that you have to figure out. And so for eight years you grow together.

The children make their own books. They create their own literature. And they find *reading* their own literature the easiest thing in the world — because it comes from the inside out. If a child cannot read in our school, we work with him to see what else he *can* do. And we work on that a lot. He can *sing* or he can play music or he can draw beautiful pictures. And we work with that until the moment when *he* decides to read. And then *he* reads, to us. In this way the children grow strong in their confidence.

The main material is taught in a two-hour stretch of time in the morning. The academic work is in the morning when the children are awake and the teachers are awake. Then we try to flow through the rest of the day with much artistic activity. The children are very lively.

I taught a class for eight years, and I ran into some of the girls in the hall today. They were quite surprised that their teacher could get dressed up and look decent enough to "go out" in the world! I said, "I'm going to talk about you a lot at Carnegie Hall," and they said, "Please *don't!*" I said, "Ohhh, remember, remember the second grade," and they got fear on their faces. And then they lightened up when they realized I wasn't *really* going to tell you what happened in the second grade!

These children were strong, sturdy, healthy children. A mother described these children in an interview as "having creative leadership potential." And I had a whole class of children with creative leadership potential! And in the kindergartens when I first went to just look at the children and try to see whether I would be able to take on such a job, some of them were under the cupboards, and some of them were under the chairs, and some of them were out in the halls, and some of them had run into the little bathrooms...because *they* knew who I was. And I said (to myself), "This is the group I want." So the first day of school they came and sat down in lovely little wooden chairs at lovely little wooden desks in lovely little rows and I thought, "Of course, this is what children love to do."

After about 15 minutes sitting at these desks they started wiggling, and I started learning how to teach.

Now we have a very fine possibility to learn about Man through history and fairy tales, as well as through current events. The classic literature is available to us. But we have the freedom to choose within this literature curriculum, this history curriculum, what actually will meet this individual child's needs, or this group of children, — what will speak to them, to their hearts, so that they will know who they are when we finish the story.

We tell stories and try not to read them. It's a very interesting thing — if you've experienced the difference when you tell a story or read a story — because the interaction is so strong in "telling" that you're building this bond.

Mathematics? Through all the different ways of trying to find the mystery of numbers, the mystery of fractions: Cake, pizza, whatever the teacher loves the best, starting with cutting it into fractions. And you find these metabolic ways, if you're a teacher like me, to find these ways to teach whatever the children need to know.

Now, if you've done your job rightly, whenever the children are in the eighth grade they say, "Mrs. Young, you're so weeiirrdd!" And then you know that they are ready to move on.

And if you've done your job right, and the student feels comfortable with the practical arts, they will feel... I...CAN...DO...ANYTHING. I can be *anybody.* I can go anywhere. I can stand on my feet in the world and I can make a difference.

◆

Now, at the end of the day when our visitors were finished with their inspection, I sat down with them. And I wasn't sure what they would have found in the various places because a variety of things could have happened. I thought perhaps it would be the music or the painting... and we sat together and I said, "Well?" They shook their heads and began to look very doubtful, and I thought, "Oh, Lord, what did they see?!" And they said, "The problem is you seem to like the children."

I'm not kidding, that's what they said. And they said, "Furthermore, you seem to like each other." And they said they had actually *seen us talking in the halls together.* They thought that was the most astonishing thing that could not be translated to the New York public school system.

I think we are in the belly of the dragon. I think we led ourselves there. Maybe *out of fear of being on the outside* of the dragon because they are so ugly. We have to get together to lead ourselves and our children out. We connected with some of John Gatto's ideas in relationship to young people finding their way in the world through apprenticeships, through community service, through a connection with the world. In our quiet valley in upstate New York it's critical that we help some young people come to adulthood with the confidence they are with us in the way *out.* We can't do it unless we join hands with all the rest who see that.

We feel that if it, the dragon, has come even to Columbia County, and we can see it, that the hour is probably late and we must move together. ◆

(CONTINUED FOLLOWING PAGE 62)

Uncogging The Wheel

by Roland Legiardi-Laura

" Roland is taking too much time, Roland interferes with other children during their work, Roland was slow today, all the other children finished before him...Roland seems to be interested in other things during his exercises. "

ood evening, everyone, it's a pleasure to see you all here and share this slice of history that's being written tonight. It's my privilege to be the one to close out the first half of our program. It's actually a wonderful irony that I am up on this stage in white tie tonight. The last time I was at Carnegie formally I wasn't permitted up on stage. It was for the Stuyvesant High School Commencement exercise, and the year was 1970. A group of us were protesting the killings at Kent State and the invasion of Cambodia. In an act of defiance we came to graduate dressed in our gym shorts. The administration was not amused and refused to let us up on stage to accept our diplomas. It's amazing what a change in style can do for one's reputation.

When John Gatto asked me to speak here, he said, "You know, Roland, you're going to have to write a speech." I protested, saying that I'd never written a speech before in my life. "Don't worry," he said, "Just condense your entire educational experience to fifteen minutes, and make it as personal and intimate as possible, while still being relevant to everyone in the audience." So here goes...

First a bit about myself: I was born and raised here on Manhattan's upper West Side. I was an only child, and my parents were European immigrants. My mother, a fashion model and jet-setter before there were jets, settled down when I was born and devoted herself to raising me. My father, a foreign correspondent during the Second World War, had a restless intellect and changed careers as often as I changed diapers. During my childhood he worked as a translator, a journalist, a private eye, a chef in an Italian restaurant and a puppeteer in a marionette theater. We never had much money, but I never really felt poor.

I attended public school in my neighborhood from kindergarten on.

I remember my first year at school quite well. The classroom was big and well lit. There were maybe 20 or 25 of us in class. School only went till noon, and we had two teachers, Miss Parker and Miss Smith. I don't remember being taught very much formally. But we had lots of crayons, paints, construction paper, clay, wooden blocks, and musical instruments. Our teachers read us stories and took us on class trips to Central Park and the Museum of Natural History. The class was a rainbow mix of cultures, and my two teachers were young, full of energy and cared about us.

I can remember learning three big lessons that year. The first was a lesson about death and responsibility. We had a goldfish bowl in class, and each day I'd watch Miss Parker feed the fish until one day I decided to feed them myself. Being of Italian/Jewish background I naturally wanted them to eat more. Well, that afternoon one of the fish was found floating, belly-up. I'd emptied half a can of fish food into the bowl... The teachers handled it with sensitivity but I remember crying bitterly in class and feeling sad for a long time.

The second lesson came at the hands of the class bully. He took great pleasure each day in knocking over my wooden block buildings. One day I grabbed him, threw him to the floor and punched him in the eye. He came to school the next morning with a black eye and his mother. I was scolded for hitting him, but he never bothered anyone again.

The third lesson, in the art of romance, came from my mother. It's a piece of wisdom that to this day I believe is in practice universally and is probably the source of most of the trouble in relationships. I was having problems with two girls in class, Maria and Barbara. Maria it seemed liked me very much, too much, and I didn't like her. She wasn't convinced by my rejection and chased me around the classroom every chance she had. Barbara on the other hand didn't seem to know I was alive, and was not at all impressed by my gifts of finger paintings and snack pretzels. I explained the situation to my mother and the advice she offered was revelatory to say the least. She suggested I start chasing Maria whenever she came close to me and that I completely ignore Barbara. In disbelief, I followed my mother's instructions and inside of a week, Maria, repulsed by my advances had found a new beau, and Barbara was pushing other girls aside to hold my hand on class trips. All in all, kindergarten was a positive experience.

Something strange began to happen in first grade. The school was starting to sort us out. I wasn't really aware of what it meant then, but I remember my mother telling me that I was being put into a special class for bright children. They called it an IGC class back then. That meant Intellectually Gifted Children. My mother seemed proud and pleased that I was in this class, but I remember her telling my father about how she hated going to the PTA meetings with all those "pushy, aggressive" mothers and how it was a "clique" of parents who decided the makeup of these special classes.

School started, and I liked my new teacher. Her name was Mrs. Cohen, and she was very warm and a grandmother to all of us. She told us all that we were her special children and that she was going to teach us how to read and write and do arithmetic. My mother, bless her anally retentive soul, saved all my exercise books, and looking through them the other day I noticed a few interesting things. The first is that I received lots of red checks and stars which seemed to indicate that I was doing well. These little marks were my first experiences with being graded. But sprinkled in with those red checks and stars of excellence were a stream of brief comments: Roland is taking too much time, Roland interferes with other children during the work, Roland was slow today, all the other children finished before him...Roland seems to be interested in other things during his exercises. So here's this $6^{1}/_2$ year-old boy with terminally messy hair and a shirt that would never stay tucked in anywhere, being told that he's too slow at doing an exercise, not focusing, disrupting the class and yet, I also seemed to be getting plenty of those red checks and stars. Hold this image in your mind for a while, and let's move on.

In second grade, the checks and stars were replaced with numbers from one to ten, and we started having little tests in class. We were given report cards with grades ranging from unsatisfactory to excellent, and there was space on the report cards for the teachers to write brief comments.

My second grade teacher was nicknamed Mrs. Dynamite; she was strict and harsh, and I filled ten notebooks that year with classroom exercises and homework. She even gave us homework over the Christmas and Easter holidays. I was still getting those checks and stars and tens for a perfect test score. The comments were the same too. Roland does not seem interested in his class work. By junior high school the ratings had been replaced with numerical averages and teachers' comments were eliminated. Finally, when I attended high school my grades were computed numerically to three decimal points. I knew exactly where I stood in a class of 750 hormonally charged 15-year-old males each day of the year. I was told that my goal in life was to attend the college of my choice, and that the surest way to achieve that goal was to get the highest grades possible. The effect on me and my peers was electric. We became our grades.

Despite the constant mixed messages and the official policy line that grades were only crude indicators at best of a person's merit, everyone knew that each and every point higher that you scored on a test brought you that much closer to the college of your dreams. An instant hierarchy was created, and everyone jostled everyone else to grab an edge. Kids would argue with their teachers about a test score. Parents would come in demanding that their son's classes be changed to another teacher who was an easy grader. Students started preparing for their SAT's with after-school classes in ninth grade. And cheating was a frowned upon but common occurrence.

I learned how to test well during those years at Stuyvesant High School. I spent 20 percent of my class time taking tests and 50 percent of my study time preparing for them. I learned how to score high. It wasn't hard if you understood the basic principles of testing. I could teach them all to you now in about 20 minutes. I would do it tonight if we had the time. I graduated with highest honors from the city's most respected public high school. And I felt sick inside. I hadn't mastered my subjects. I simply knew how to answer questions.

I remember I had a particularly hard time with Trigonometry — I just didn't get it. My class average over the semester was 32, 65 was passing, and I needed to get at least an 85 in order to save my overall average. I went up to my math teacher one day after class and bet him that I could score over 90 on the State Regents Trig Exam. He laughed, said I was nuts but promised to give me whatever I scored on the exam as my final grade. For two weeks before the test I went to bed at night with my eyes open and the lights on. I had plastered the walls of my room with trig formulas. I scored 91 on the exam. My teacher kept his word, and two days later I had forgotten everything.

◆

I remember always feeling rushed in school. The teachers were rushed, the course texts were impossible to cover in one semester, so class work was always abbreviated. You couldn't ask too many questions, there wasn't enough time, and while most of the teachers were willing to answer questions after class, you had only four minutes between classes. You felt awkward if you asked too many questions. Other kids would accuse you of trying to suck up to the teacher, and surely there were kids who made sucking up their profession. The tension was palpable in the halls, in the lunch room, in the bathrooms and on the stairways. Kids cracked, teachers cracked too. One geometry teacher gave an entire class the square root of 2 as a final grade. A classmate of mine whose father happened to be the student body college advisor — in other words a god — managed to get accepted to Harvard although his grades didn't quite predict such good fortune. His first semester home from the big H for the holidays he jumped out of a twenty-story window rather than tell his father he was failing.

What was I being prepared for back in first grade when my kindly teacher started giving me checks and stars? What strange addiction to someone else's numerical equivalent of my soul was I being hooked onto as a six-year-old? And what was anyone really learning about me by assigning these numbers? What I learned about myself was clear and painful.

Another perverted lesson that was being taught to me in school was that smart kids seemed invariably to be white. Nothing David Duke is saying in Louisiana tonight, no racist message he ever delivered to his followers was more subtly or effectively inscribed onto the hearts of children than the message of the tracking system. With the single exception of kindergarten, every grade I attended in public school had attached to it some Orwellian acronym symbolizing genetic superiority. IGC: Intellectually Gifted Children, SP: Special Progress, SPE: Special Progress Enriched, Gifted and Talented. Even if you accept the absurd notion that those kinds of distinctions between kids can be made, how can you explain that in my twelve years of schooling on Manhattan's upper West Side, where 85 percent of public school kids are non-white, there was never a black or latino in any of my classes. We were taught, without a word ever being said, to fear and despise those kids, and they were taught to loathe themselves and envy us. Tracking continues unabated in schools today. Elite private schools are no better, they just have sharper public relations offices.

But let me pass through my anger and frustration for just a moment now as I believe I was actually invited to speak here tonight about the positive. What events, conditions and people in my life gave me the tools and the strength to recover from the effects of my formal education? (I must be beginning to sound like some crazed member of a new 12-step program: Pupil's Anonymous) But the answer is quite simple: My parents, my friends and my own stubborn streak.

First my parents: I learned from my parents in two ways. By watching them and by their active support. Observation of one's family for the most part is unconscious. You adopt your parents' gestures, the way they speak, walk, stand effortlessly. As you get older you come to understand them as people and you learn from them how they measure themselves, what they see as real success and real failure. This often has nothing to do with what your parents actually say to you about what is right and wrong, good and bad, important or insignificant, but rather it is developing a sense of who your parents are as whole people.

My father taught me two great lessons — the first, from his strong side, was that I could do anything I wanted to do. And that I enjoy doing it was the important thing. The second, harder lesson from his weak side was that I needed to finish what I started.

My father also read to me and told me stories almost every night of my childhood. Most of what he read and told me were from Roman and Greek history and mythology. What I think that did was leave me with a sense of place and history and gave me a point of departure from which to measure my own time and culture.

My mother taught me how to laugh — perhaps the most important tool of survival anyone can have. She was also the indulgent and over-protective mother that is the curse of every "only" child. But out of this indulgence, she gave me a great gift: my privacy and the time to use it. Looking back over those old report cards, I realized that I stayed home from school on average 25 percent of every school year, a record 52 days during the reign of Mrs. Dynamite. I wasn't a sickly child, I just didn't like going to school, and my mom obliged by writing an excuse whenever I wanted one. I remember spending a lot of time at home reading and playing with toy soldiers.

From my friends I learned how to live life. And amongst my friends I include my teachers, those rare people who found a way to share their knowledge with me. It's magic when it happens, it's invisible, and it's quite natural. There are many fine teachers in the world. They are people who have a graceful and delicate touch, and their gift is given unconditionally. It can be your lover, who with one small whisper uncouples you from your troublesome ego. Or it can be someone like John Gatto who manages to convince you time and again that you are your own best teacher, and that the world can indeed be changed.

Thank you all. I think it's time now for a well-deserved, if brief, break.   ◆

My Life As A Troublemaker

By Jamaal M. Watson

"I understand Senator Kerrey is running for President ...does the time he spent with us troublemakers reflect badly on him, or does it reflect badly on schoolpeople?"

Welcome to the second half of our program. My name is Jamaal Watson, and together with my buddy Victor, I'm the creator of "Elvis Impersonator." If you went to our school records you might find us listed as "troublemakers" and "below average" in many subjects. And if you went around the whole country you would find millions of kids set down in secret records the same way.

Why do schools do that? What's it supposed to *mean*? Do the words "troublemaker" and "below average" tell you anything useful? Earlier this year Senator Bob Kerrey of Nebraska asked Victor and me to breakfast at the Algonquin Hotel... He listened to our analysis of what's wrong with schools for *three hours.* No school official or school reformer ever asked our opinion on anything before, but I understand Senator Kerrey is running for President...does the time he spent with us troublemakers reflect badly on *him*, or does it reflect badly on schoolpeople?

Let me tell you a few other things about Victor and myself that schools don't know...and wouldn't care about if they did. Together we talked Annie Nocenti, the great Marvel comic book creator, into a personal apprenticeship. Each week we snuck out of school to her studio for private lessons in storytelling. (Mr. Gatto covered for us.) Victor was written about in *The Christian Science Monitor*...I won three citywide essay contests and got a job as a consultant...paying $15 an hour. Victor and I visited 20 different engineering companies to watch how they did their work. You won't find *that* in our school records, but you may find us called "troublemakers." Victor and I took a second day off each week to go to the public library by ourselves. I think we learned as much there as we did in all eight years of school put together. Yes, we had to sneak out to do it...yes, Mr. Gatto covered for us again. I think he must have trusted us to use the time wisely...schools aren't supposed to do that, of course.

What kind of business is hated by its customers...and dislikes its customers in return?! Only one...it's called "school." Take a walk to your local school and look at it closely — who would put a kid in such a place and ring bells in his ears if they liked him? Have you ever noticed how few adult people ever talk about their own school days or even remember them? Shouldn't 12 years make more memories...if they were good years?...

◆

The Healthy Side Of Exhaustion

By Dave Lehman

> " There is a second kind of exhaustion — that deep feeling of satisfaction after successful completion of a challenge...it is the exhaustion of the athlete at the end of the event... "

O urs is *not* an "exhausted school"! Our school is alive and well, growing and changing. There are two kinds of "exhaustion" here — one is the exhaustion of defeat, discouragement, and despair, of frustrating, unsuccessful, unrewarded efforts; the exhaustion of a totally worn-out building in which little works, where there are holes in the ceiling, broken windows, unrepairable plumbing, and faulty furnaces — indeed exhaustion. Then there is a second kind of "exhaustion" — that deep feeling of satisfaction after the successful completion of a challenge, of a job well done at the end of a full expenditure of one's total energies and commitment; it is the exhaustion of the athlete at the end of the event; it is the feeling at the end of class when you know there was real learning going on! It is this second kind of exhaustion that I feel, and that our staff often feels. So let me tell you something about our school, about the Alternative Community School of Ithaca, New York — a *public* middle school and high school.

In our eighteenth year as a *public school of choice,* we serve the whole School District of Ithaca, which is the most diverse upstate community outside of the big cities. While working with students whose parents are employed at Cornell University and Ithaca College, we also serve a 155 square mile rural population, being the northern most county of Appalachia; and we have an approximately equal representation of students from our school district's 20 percent minority population of African-Americans, Asians, Latin Americans, Native Americans, and others. In addition, 10 percent of our students are officially classified as "Learning Disabled or Emotionally Disturbed", and another 15 to 25 percent each year are identified as "PSEN", Pupils with Special Education Needs, being behind in one or more basic skill areas by at least a year. Students freely apply to ACS and are admitted from our waiting list as soon as room becomes available by means of a lottery drawing from our different applicant pools to assure we maintain our diversity. As a public school we are funded at the same basic per pupil cost as the two other middle schools and the central high school in Ithaca. Thus, we are staffed based on the same basic district-wide formula of one full-time teacher equivalent for every 18.65 students. (Those .65 students are the ones that seem hardest to work with though — they never quite seem to be all there!)

Now, with that quick background about our school district and our student population, let me describe what it is that these students have chosen in coming to ACS, the kinds of reforms and changes that we have made at the Alternative Community School, because I want you to know that schools — indeed *public* schools — *can* be different; they *can* be changed; there *are* other ways of doing school that can be highly successful. I would highlight *three key features* that make ACS a genuine alternative, a real choice for sixth through twelfth graders in Ithaca.

First, we are a democratically run school, a laboratory in civics where students and staff (and to the degree that their time permits — parents) are directly and regularly involved in the day-to-day decision-making of running our school. For example, some two years ago a proposal came before our weekly All School Town Meeting — which incidentally is run by our student Agenda Committee — that "community service" become a graduation requirement, and our total student body and staff, after much discussion, overwhelmingly voted their approval for a minimum of 30 hours of community service becoming a new graduation requirement. I suggest that is real shared decision-making, a real sharing of power.

Secondly, we strive to personalize education at ACS, to work with each student holistically, not just with their intellectual abilities and difficulties, but their emotional, social, and physical selves as well; to get to know, to work and play, to laugh and cry with them as total human beings, to take them seriously for who they are. Here we have used our resources to develop an average class size of 16 to foster this kind of personalization and have created "Family Groups" of about 12 students each with one teacher, where that teacher meets at least twice a week with the whole group, serving as their advisor, their advocate, their facilitator of interpersonal growth, and the main contact with their parents.

Thirdly, we have developed a program and a curriculum which has *five major options* by which students may learn, recognizing what works for one student doesn't always work for another. *One*, there are "classes or courses," both for our middle school and our high school students, which meet four times per week, either for a single 45-minute period or for a double period, often interdisciplinary, as in English and social studies for courses in Facing History or Medieval Times. These classes may be for just one nine-week cycle as is typical of our middle school, or semester or year-long in our high school program, and they are more relevant, not from a State syllabus, but developed by the teachers with their students, such as a course last winter on the "Persian Gulf War." *Two*, we have "Extended Project" blocks in our weekly schedule, all Tuesday afternoons and all Thursday mornings to do different kinds of things that work well in longer time blocks of an hour and 15 minutes to three and half hours, such as "Creative Writing" out in the greater Ithaca community, computer programming, ceramics, ice skating, video production, bicycling, or "Outing Challenge," an Outward Bound type of program done cooperatively with staff from our local Youth Bureau. *Three*, is our "Community Studies Program" in which students are placed individually with adults in various businesses, social agencies, or college departments, "learning by doing" either as career exploration experiences or for actual academic credit. For example, a young seventh grade girl who thinks she would like to become a veterinarian has a community placement with a local veterinarian — and incidentally may learn that she hates the sight of blood and doesn't want to become a vet — certainly less costly than discovering that after the first year of grad school! Or a high school junior learning bookkeeping and accounting for math credit through a cooperative arrangement between one of our math teachers, our Coordinator of Community Studies, and a staff member at a local Credit Union. *Four*, students, even sixth-graders!, have the opportunity to do "Independent Studies," one-on-one with a teacher to explore in depth a subject of keen personal interest. Such studies may result not only in a research paper, but a videotape, or a play, a laboratory or field experiment, a photographic essay, or any one of a number of other ways of demonstrating learning. And *five,* our students may complete parts of their educational program by learning at another educational institution in Ithaca, not only Cornell or Ithaca college where some of our high schoolers take courses, but a local ballet studio, a karate center, or our Community School of Music and Art. The *overriding idea* is to find ways of learning that will work for each student. Even within our heterogeneous, non-tracked, non-graded middle school and high school classes or courses, our teachers strive to find different ways of working with the different learning styles of our individual students. And where there are classes which have students who are having particular difficulties, we will add a second teacher, specifically trained to focus on and assist the learning of these students as a support to the subject matter teacher.

But what evidence is there — you ask — that our students are successful? How do we know the changes we have made — the reforms, the different ways of doing things — really work? I offer three indicators of our success: *one,* our waiting list and our growth from a junior high of 60 students to a middle school and high school of 260; *two,* performance of our students even on conventional standardized tests which is comparable or better than their counterparts in Ithaca's other secondary schools; and *three,* our high school graduates — and we have had twelve graduating classes — an average of 85 percent go to colleges across the country either immediately after high school or within three years of their graduation, others become fully employed, and none are on welfare or in prison.

All of this has not gone unnoticed by our local Central Administration and School Board, for they are increasingly interested in what we are doing, as are the teachers and administrators in the other secondary schools in Ithaca as they look to make reforms in their own programs. At the state level, we have just become one of the first group of schools in the New York State Education Department's "Partnership Schools Program" being designed as a major means of supporting the implementation of the Board of Regents approved Commissioner's "New Compact for Learning." And this has come about largely through our involvement nationally as one of approximately 100 schools who are full members of the "Coalition of Essential Schools," spearheaded by Ted Sizer of Brown University.

But I'm not here just to speak about our school, but to speak about the need for fundamental educational reform in this country and about public schools of choice. Things *can* be different in public education; our public schools *can* change. Indeed, many schools and communities have already made or begun to make major, fundamental changes. There are relevant, motivating, self-esteem building ways of helping all young people become critical thinking problem-solvers. There are more authentic ways of evaluating learning than outmoded conventional, standardized paper and pencil tests. And, yes, there was a point when I homeschooled my own children for part of one of their elementary years in rural Ohio, and, yes, I did co-found a non-public, independent alternative school in rural Texas, at least partly for my own children, again in their elementary years. But supporting such different ways of educating as these were relatively easy for me as a white, middle class, slightly balding, definitely graying male with a PhD. And I *do* believe in the importance of such opportunities; yet, for the overwhelming majority of our population, it is the public schools which *must* change, and *can* change, and at least some *are changing* as evidenced by our school. And in order for public schools of choice, like ACS, to be positive contributors to this desperately-needed change in the schools of *this* city, *this* state, and *this* country, then the following conditions, which are true for our school, *must* be met:

First, there must be real choices among essentially equal schools that are funded by the same per pupil expenditures.

Secondly, there must be real access to all of these schools of choice, which means not only free public transportation to such schools, but real communication to all students and their parents about such choices and the process of admission, communication that is not dependent solely on a written letter sent home.

Thirdly, each school of choice must guarantee a fully diverse student population made up of representatives of all of the minorities within a given school district, from all of the economic sectors of that district, and from students with learning difficulties as well.

Fourthly, there must be real democratic control of such a school of choice by the administration, staff, students, and parents.

For as important as it is that our schools become more humane places, reorganized, and with major changes in their curricula, textbooks, teaching philosophies and methodologies, and with more direct involvement and even direct control by those being served by our schools, changes such as those I've described about ACS — the most fundamental change that also must occur, and *occur now*, is the elimination of our dual system of "separate and unequal" education. There *must* be a more equitable redistribution of funds to level the playing field of education. And this will not be brought about by treating schools as competing businesses, for the free-market dynamics will not work to correct these inequities and injustices found particularly in our urban and rural schools, rather they will work to deepen these divisions even more. Although money, or the lack of money, is a major factor in this inequity, making money available to foster even more the existing private and parochial school choices, will only serve to weaken our public schools at the very moment when they show the greatest signs and potential for real change. Businesses can, however, increasingly be helpful in providing sites for "mini-apprenticeships," career explorations, and other "learning by doing" experiences as in our ACS Community Studies programs. They can be helpful in making it easy for their employees to have release time to attend conferences at school with their youngsters' teachers, and by providing funding to equalize the quality of education and the physical facilities of all our schools.

For things *can* be done; and you and I must, I say *must*, do them! It is for all the children of this nation and for their futures — we can do no less. It is toward *this* end that we must *exhaust* all of our efforts, particularly in a democracy, in a land still waiting for "liberty and justice for all." ◆

Breaking The Rules

by Barbara Jill Cummings

" In Brazil I found new teachers of a type never given credence by our educational systems. My teachers were peasant farmers, Indian chiefs, rubber tappers, rural union leaders. Most of them were illiterate, and all of them taught me... "

When John asked me to speak, he said it was because he wanted my own experience with both traditional and alternative education, and because of what I made of it, despite the odds.

It was something I had thought of often. I have no doubts in my mind that my first exposure to alternative education with John Gatto played a pivotal role in my awakening of what education could, and should, be for young people growing up in an increasingly complicated and challenging world community.

For years as a student, I went through my own monotonous routine of education as discipline and education as conformity. In fact, my own deviance from the traditional and "appropriate" role of students resulted in great frustration in my life and alienation from many "educators" in the public school system.

At times this frustration took the form of requests to my family to take me out of school because I was too repressed there; at other times it took the form of increased discipline and academic penalties *against* me.

Regardless of the measures that the traditional educational system took to cope with "deviant" students like myself, the obvious root of the problem lay in the inability of the schools to respond to my insistent demands for real-life experience. And for learning that was relevant to my experiences outside of the school.

Because I have been asked not to expound on a philosophy of "education in general," of which I most definitely hold strong views, I will relate to you some of my own personal experiences in searching for an education which could help me to understand, and to effectively *influence*, the world in which I found myself growing up, in New York — and, also, in the global community I began to search out as early as I was able.

Speakers tonight have referred to the advantage of "home schooling," to which I was exposed from a very early age, as a complement to my public schooling. My family took an active interest in my learning and exposed me to what were, consciously or unconsciously, fundamentally different philosophies of learning from those that I encountered in school. When studying history I was referred at home to alternative texts, books such as the *People's History of the United States*, which challenged the Columbus-centered view of America with the Native American perspective, for example.

I consider this involvement of my family fortunate, but I would not look to it as the answer to flaws in our education, because the demands on most families are already burdensome. I would look instead to alternative models of institutionalized schooling, which absolutely must be incorporated into public education if we are to meet the challenges of a changing world.

◆

I began early to search for educational experiences which could help me adjust to and affect the society in which I found myself. John Gatto's Lab School, at the time located at Intermediate School 44 on 77th Street, provided my first venture in applying my understanding of the world to practical actions —ranging from making a living to conducting city planning evaluations to beginning the process of critical review of traditional education — which continues here tonight.

For years after leaving the Lab School, I was grateful for my experiences there, while simultaneously cursing John Gatto for making me *unfit* for my necessary return to discipline-oriented traditional schooling.

I attended four years of high school at one of New York's most competitive public education institutions, an experience which prepared me less for living in society than that one year I spent investigating the city at 13 years old. In fact, I nearly did not finish high school because of my frustration over wasting time when there were "things to be done." The way I remember it, I stormed out of high school in my last year, vowing never to return. An appeal to the administration from my family made it clear to them that my forced return would result in my institutionalization, for which they would be held responsible. I spent the rest of that year settling into my own home and a full-time job. I only returned at the end of the year for graduation ceremonies (from which I somehow emerged with honors).

Once the required penance time in mandatory education was over, I began searching for educational options that would allow me creative scope in learning. I spent my college years studying in Panama and in Kenya, and working in positions that took me to Australia, Hawaii, and the hidden sectors of my own community. I spent my month in Panama camped in the jungle, studying Tamarin monkeys (who were wonderful teachers). My three months in Kenya were spent in a tent on a wild game reserve and traveling to meet with Maasai herdsmen. I worked for the government's Fish and Wildlife Department in Hawaii.

I finally settled into a college that made human sense to me while providing rigorous and challenging hurdles to further test my ideas and world views. As a student, I taught, became an academic activist, and finally secured funding for a senior thesis that took me to the Amazon in Brazil to investigate influences of development projects on local environments and populations. For three months, I traveled through the Amazon by boat, bus and flatbed truck (with a roped bull for company) and spoke with people who were struggling to survive in a country that had essentially forgotten them. This work was the culmination of years of attempting to mesh my academic, philosophical, and activist interests into a life work that I continue to pursue today.

My own successful search for a creative, challenging educational environment, (which I found at Hampshire College in Amherst, Massachusetts) was crucial to the life I have today. I recently published my first book, which dealt with the investigation of the Amazon I began in college. In addition to representing the culmination of one stage in my development, this work began an entirely new, and still more enriching phase in my continued search for creative learning.

In Brazil I found new teachers of a type never given credence by our educational systems. My teachers were peasant farmers, Indian chiefs, rubber tappers, rural union leaders. Most of them were illiterate, and all of them taught me more in three months than I could have hoped for in all my 16 years of schooling. My most influential teacher, Paiakan Kaiapo — political chief of a Kayapo Indian village — was arrested while I was in Brazil, for attempting to change government policy regarding development of his own lands. I myself was run out of Brazil by government agents for listening to the voices of teachers such as he.

We have still not recognized the value of this type of learning by living. No "system" of education can provide that if it does not include self-learning, creative investigation, and independence, both to make mistakes and to discover new truths. Our teachers need to be guides to experience, not enforcers of doctrine and discipline and must encourage us to pursue a goal of becoming "citizens of the world," which may be enacted locally or internationally, but must above all be informed, *not* sheltered, and *not* misled.

When I consider the most important lesson I taught myself through my years of searching for an education, it is that it is not only okay, but essential to learn how to BREAK THE RULES. I continue to break the rules. If I ever tire of doing this, at that time I will cease to learn.　　◆

Learning Flows Naturally

by Mary Leue

"
And yet, both as parents and as teachers, we teach *who we are*, not just what we think or what we give children to do."

I want to start with a kind of footnote. What most of you may not know is that about three weeks ago John presented a magnificent workshop in Albany on the day before his keynote speech at the State Association of School Boards conference. Chris Mercogliano, the co-director of our school, was all set to give John a glowing introduction — but John, being John, and not knowing that, just dove in and started ahead on his own. So I'd like to deliver Chris' introduction for him. I think it's a terrific statement about John, too good to waste. Chris wrote it out for me, so here it is:

The other day I found myself telling some of the younger kids at school the old folk tale "The Emperor's New Clothes." You probably remember that it was a child in the village who cried out, "He has nothing on at all," thereby breaking the thick spell of denial being paraded by the emperor and all of his loyal — and frightened — subjects. Well, there is a magical child alive and well inside John Gatto who is the source of his giftedness as a teacher, and who is now hell-bent on seeing to it that our schools do not grind the magic out of yet another generation of our children. John is a man with a mission, and I pray that the spell that has settled over our teachers and our educational institutions has not already become so widespread that it cannot be broken. If anyone can do it, John and his growing band of merry men and women can!

In the sense that Chris is using the term, I believe we are all magical children, now grown up. It is to be hoped that we still remember our childhoods and thus can stay open to allowing *our* children to grow up living out their magical heritage, not just grow up to become unconscious products of our own pasts as so many adults have done. And in this context, I need here to pay a special tribute to my most important personal teachers — my mother and father, the two most remarkable people I have ever known. They read to us throughout all the years of our childhood, taught us wilderness skills, recognition of birds, wild plants and trees, and geological features of the land. With them we went camping, ocean sailing, mountain-climbing, rock-climbing, and skiing. From them I have learned whatever I may have of love of learning, respect for childhood, courage, integrity, curiosity, persistence, discrimination, and cultural breadth. It was at their insistence that I graduated from high school on the high honor roll, from Bryn Mawr College with an A.B. degree, and from the Children's Hospital School of Nursing in Boston, Massachusetts. Their lessons are still bearing fruit for me.

At our school we recognize our debts to many educators from the past who understood this: such as the eighteenth century thinker Jean Jacques Rousseau; his contemporary, the Swiss Johann Heinrich Pestalozzi, whose beliefs were brought to America by Joseph Neef in 1808; Friedrich Froebel, who worked with and adopted Pestalozzi's insights about childhood as the basis for his concept of children as needing to grow like flowers in a carefully tended garden — a garden of children. The rich experiences provided for children by the Waldorf schools that follow the teachings of Rudolph Steiner are another source from which we draw, as well as the insights of Maria Montessori and John Dewey. Most immediately, we take inspiration from the self-regulatory libertarianism of A.S. Neill and the humanistic insights into the souls of the children of the ghetto contained in the writings of George Dennison.

We believe that working with children demands a trained and very keen eye and ear attuned to one's inner truth as well as a willingness to live in the child's own world as a participant observer. In the world that is emerging around us, this need for self-knowledge seems to us to go all too often unmet. We believe it is this unmet need to know ourselves at a deep level which is the chief missing ingredient in a cultural dilemma that is approaching crisis stage as our traditional support systems — the family and the community — break down at an accelerating rate. We are becoming inundated as a society by a tidal wave of acute problems such as alcoholism, drug addiction, criminality and psychosis — as well as characterological problems like narcissism, sociopathy, neurosis and chronic physiological imbalances of all sorts.

This breakdown process has been defined as arising from the neglect of feelings — the grief, rage and fear — felt by the neglected inner child and it has been suggested that it is this neglect which creates such havoc in our adult lives. This might be called the negative side of the magic of childhood. The damage even involves our societal patterns of giving birth — not just the education of our children in schools. Michel Odent, a French research-minded obstetrician has had many years of working with, rather than against, the wisdom of the natural body during birth. His work demonstrates the madness of our technologized system of obstetrical management which has resulted in nearly half of all hospital births ending in Cesarean section. It is to this entire range of issues that we in our school and our community are attempting to address ourselves.

Thus, during the 22 years of our existence, we have grown from a handful of parents who had a dream of democratic education and started a little school in the inner city of Albany in 1969, to a multi-generational community with the school as its center. Everything we have grown to be in those two-plus decades has come into being in response to needs we have experienced as essential to a model of life that makes sense in human terms, a model that works. In this process we have grown rich! No, not in monetary terms, but in the real values that make life a vital experience.

Our school is one of the oldest urban free schools in the country. In the setting of this all-embracing community, the Free School is far more a community center and less a traditional institution. We don't select children; we accept whoever comes. Similarly, we don't hire teachers; we accept whoever comes. Then we teach them how to be with us. Our community has a simple criterion for evaluating those who are drawn to us: namely, that they take us seriously enough to come, stay and learn. Most of our teachers have lived in the community for ten years or more.

Learning flows naturally out of the community atmosphere and is

much less a goal in itself. Skills learning —which the children love —
takes very little time in the total scheme, and activities such as putting
on plays, making puppets, singing, doing sports, watching movies,
reading out loud, playing games, and doing crafts, take up most of it.
The adults have as much fun as the children, and staff burnout is
unknown among us. One very important element we offer our children,
both by experience and by example, is an awareness that "You can do
it!" Children who leave us after two or three years have a rare natural
sense of confidence, dignity and leadership.

But the school is only one setting for the learning activities in which
our children are involved, just as we, the adults in the community, are
only some of the people from whom our kids are free to learn or take
inspiration. We have a small farm in the community, and kids help take
care of our animals. We have two hundred acres of wilderness land
recently donated to the school which is now part of our lives and will
be even more so as time goes by and our presence there becomes even
more a daily part of who we are.

Wilhelm Reich said, "Love, work and knowledge are the well-
springs of life. They should also govern it." The principles by which our
community lives and by which it is governed are indeed love, work and
knowledge. Two things could be said to define us as a community: *work
democracy* and *total mutual support* for families.

The term *work democracy*, coined by Reich, is used to describe crite-
ria for community on the basis of need and obligation. It is a pragmatic
definition of peer-level status among adults and between adults and
children, both in the community and in the school.

Total mutual support means that everyone in the community plays
roles usually assigned to specialists. That has meant taking on many
more roles than most people think of doing, as a way of simplifying our
lives as a community. We all teach, take care of one another's children,
doctor them, take responsibility for their behavior, look upon them as
our joint responsibility. We do the same things with each other, as families, and gradually we have taught ourselves how to play all of these
roles more effectively.

We have learned through experience what community problems to
tackle ourselves and what to leave to someone with specialized skills.
And we have learned ways that work better than the societally
approved ones in the crucial areas of maternity, parenting, and education. Taking over these support roles as we have has meant that our
very limited incomes go a lot further than one would expect — and that
we work very hard. But over time, we have also learned to increase our

joint prosperity and pleasure in other ways.

We have a monthly parenting support group and a cooperative pre-natal support group for pregnant couples as well as labor coaching in the hospital. And we have developed a number of additional group resources that allow us to focus on improving our relationship patterns, including personal growth and growth as couples and as parents. We have, for example, a weekly therapeutic group that serves many community functions and, most crucially, gives us a way of steadily deepening our contact with one another.

Six years ago we set up a pooled investment, insurance and loan group of the kind usually called a Mondragon group which has provided community families with improvement loans of various kinds and has also paid a large part of our teachers' medical expenses. We also have our own natural foods store at discount prices, a small bookstore, a library, and a large audio and video tape library, as well as a wooden boat-building shop and a clothing manufacturing business owned by members of the community. One of our families is also a husband-wife legal firm, and two of us who are R.N.'s as well as teachers also play the roles of barefoot doctor and triage agent.

Finding money to live on has always been a joint responsibility, since the school belongs to us all. The school doesn't really pay salaries to its teachers in the sense businesses usually mean by that term; rather, we have divided up the income, with adequate allocations for the needs of the property itself. In addition to ten buildings clustered in a two-block area of downtown Albany owned by the school (income from which constitutes about two-thirds of the school's economic base), families in some way associated with the school own an additional ten buildings in the area and consider themselves part of the Free School community.

Besides describing our school and community in terms of what we *do*, I want also to emphasize my belief that it has been important for us to understand *why* we do what we do, not just *that* we do it. We are all engaged in an on-going process of creating a model of life that includes adults in families, includes adult activities and skills practiced right in the community, and includes teaching kids adult models in both characterological and occupational forms. Like the saying attributed to Dewey, we are learning to do by doing.

So why is it important to ask why we do it? What's wrong with just doing? What's wrong is lack of awareness — or mindfulness, to use the Buddhist expression. Being members of the society of the industrialized west, most of us are functional extroverts, and as such, are largely incapable of serving as adequate models for children, we believe. Our own learned inner models of reality which operate *beneath* the level of "doing" have far more of an impact on kids than most of us feel comfortable in acknowledging, yet there is very little institutional support for becoming aware of this level of experience which comes primarily from the culture of our parents, and can only be discovered by the development of inner knowing on our own. Often acquiring such inner knowing involves a willingness to feel one's residual pain.

And yet, both as parents and as teachers, we teach *who we are*, not just what we think or what we give children to do. Many titular adults are unwilling to take this fact into account when they are dealing with children. We fail to compare what we may *think* we are teaching kids with what they are actually *getting* from us. Doing that involves a willingness to stay attuned to our inner truth no matter how painful that may be, as well as a willingness to live in the child's own world as participant observers, not just follow a model.

It is in this sense that we consider ourselves a multi-generational learning community. We take what we need to learn from our own histories to round out our experiences of ourselves as fully conscious beings; and we do our best to use the learnings derived from our individual histories to help in the process of creating a shared future for everyone both as individual families and as a community. It's not a way that works for everyone — but perhaps it is a little like what Joe Campbell says of marriage: "Marriage," he says, "is not about happiness but about transformation." Or as one of our own members said recently, "It's like having twenty lovers!" ◆

The Problem Of Schooling

by John Taylor Gatto

" Experts have consistently misdiagnosed and misdefined the problem of schooling to serve their own pocketbooks. The difficulty is not that children don't learn to read very well — it is that kids don't learn at all the way schools insist on teaching. "

Experts have consistently misdiagnosed and misdefined the problem of schooling to serve their own pocketbooks. The difficulty is not that children don't learn to read, write and do arithmetic very well — it is that kids don't learn at all the way schools insist on teaching.

When we strip children of a primary experience base — as confinement schooling must do to justify its very existence — we destroy the natural sequences of learning which always put experience first. Only much later, after a bath of experience, can the thin gruel of abstraction mean anything. We haven't forgotten this, but there is just not much profit in it for the people and the businesses who make their bread and butter from monopoly schooling. Indeed, you can't hire people who can handle primary data well as teachers because there are so many other things they *can* do — that's why science teachers are seldom scientists and other teaching "specialists" are seldom very good practitioners of what they presumably "teach."

The call you hear all around for a longer school year is only a mask over the endless longing of the school institution for a guaranteed clientele; in times like these, when money isn't forthcoming, then perhaps people can be *frightened* into handing it over. I've just given you a better way to understand why you hear so often about the wonders of Japanese schooling, twelve weeks longer than our own. You are being asked to believe that more is better at the very instant that Hong Kong, with a school year ten weeks *shorter* than Japan's, whips that nation in every single academic category measured. In New York City we hear with reasonable frequency that Israel's long school term confirms the lesson of Japan since both nations trounce U.S. student competition handily. But during this whole gruesome exercise in manipulating our national mind to prepare it for *more* schoolteaching *(in spite of* its hideous track record) I have yet to hear *once* how handily Flemish Belgium trounces Israel in every academic category — even though it has a school year *eleven weeks shorter than Israel's* and *nineteen* weeks shorter than Hong Kong's.

Have *you* heard these things before? Is it possible someone would rather you didn't? Perhaps you can think of some convincing explanation why we fail to hear of the victories of nations with short school years in the current stampede toward a longer one here.

If you would think clearly, first guard the integrity of your mind against the myths of schoolmen. The most important thing you need to know about the school hierarchy in New York City — and "official" reform initiatives endorsed by New York teacher-colleges like Columbia's, Bank Street's and Fordham's, and those of invisible 501c3 entities like "The Center for Educational Innovation" — is that they maintain a school empire of over 30,000 administrative jobs, visible ones and covert ones. Three-fourths of each school dollar goes for administrative costs. The Catholic Church oversees a million kids in parochial school with about 1/60th the number of administrative jobs New York schools have — indeed they have more administrators than every nation in western Europe combined.

Why don't *you* know that? Is it possible someone would rather you didn't?

Look at the disgrace these 30,000 experts have brought down on this city. Their existence bankrupts the middle class. Look at the nightmare world they have inflicted on our children. My own school district, a wealthy place located mainly between Columbia University and Lincoln Center, was declared in 1989 the worst single school district in New York

State — out of more than 700 "competitors"! Worst in reading, worst in math, worst in many other things. Community School District 3, which no more serves the "community" than its version of "public" education serves the public, has, on its northern boundary, Columbia University, just south of that sits the world famous Bank Street College of Education, and on its southern boundary rests Fordham University.

In my 26 years of teaching, none of these fine and arrogant institutions, none of the king's ransom in tax dollars spent by the school district, and none of the feverish rhetoric of the West Side's loud and arrogant political establishment, none of this massed wealth and wisdom has done one tiny bit to alter the nightmare destiny of the children whose minds are put to death in District 3 schools.

Come to a school board meeting in District 3 and you will find the school board and superintendent congratulating each other about the good job they have done. A spectacle I believe is repeated everywhere that monopoly schooling flourishes.

Enough. Enough. Enough. There will *be* no reform in these schools without competition. Any promise of change from within is an illusion. Government schools are a jobs project, one that hires two people for every one and a quarter needed. Government schools are the single largest form of political patronage everywhere, their sweetheart contracts with bus companies, builders, booksellers and other profiteers are legendary — in school purchasing there are no economies of scale. With their no-show, low-show jobs, their favors for insiders, and all the rest, they are corrupt places, and they are corrupting of the precious time of children. Time to declare the monopoly irrelevant.

Government schools must be made to compete for tax dollars with *every* other form of schooling, old and new. Let parents and communities *choose* what kind of education they will buy. Trust the customers, they will correct our school problem with the power of the purse string. Time to end the Soviet system of government compulsion schools that disgraces our nation and ruins our children. We need tax credits, vouchers, and some more sophisticated ways to develop thousands of entrepreneurial schools. Down in Knoxville, Tennessee, a young man named Chris Wittle is gambling 60 million dollars of his own money to come up with a new design for schooling. I've met him; I think he's going to succeed. We'll all be better for his success because it will stimulate others to try their own designs.

There is no one right way to grow up. Locked up in the minds and hearts of people everywhere are hundreds of good designs — just waiting for the incentive of free market competition, and perhaps a little underwriting at the beginning, to burst forth.

But so far the State Departments of Education, and the materials suppliers who love their sweetheart deals, and the institutes and foundations and other special interests who make a living out of school business as usual, have stopped this natural return to the successful free market in schooling that the U.S. once enjoyed.

My instincts tell me the school establishment thinks they are going to get away with it again. That's why I rented Carnegie Hall — to ask people to help me force the politicians to put school choice legislation on the ballot. Once we succeed in forcing that, the handwriting will be on the wall. And like insects exposed when a rock is lifted the 30,000 administrators will scurry to and fro vainly trying to protect their privileges. Perhaps I won't live to see that end, but I want my granddaughter Mossie to see it.

◆

I asked you earlier not to be fooled any longer by calls for a longer school year, now let me warn you against being fooled that your kids will miss anything important by scrapping this monopoly for free market choice schools. Schoolmen will tell you we need these places to take care of the poor, but the Gallup Poll will tell you it is the poorest among us who scream most loudly for choice.

Schoolmen will have you believe that no one can learn without these places even though literacy was higher in the United States *before* we built the factory school system.

Schoolmen will tell you that we can't enter the technological future without mass compulsion schooling but the tremendous computer revolution which made 45 million of us computer literate over the past 20 years owes nothing whatever to formal schooling! People taught themselves by reading instructions, watching others, begging for advice, by experimentation, by trial and error, by tuning into networks, by buying lessons from thousands of little entrepreneurs. *That's* how we learned to be computer literate — schools had nothing to do with it at all! I have a personal story to tell here — for the past 15 years I've watched a New Jersey hairdresser, a mother with young children to raise, turn herself into a high-powered executive of a freight consolidation company doing business from coast to coast. Judy Kovach, the lady this evening is dedicated to, didn't have an MBA and spent her evenings dancing instead of reading *The Wall Street Journal.* But by force of will and hard work, and by dint of a good attitude that made her a lifelong learner, she became superb at a tough, demanding job — and rose to the #2 spot in a national company, by merit. School had nothing to do with Judy's success, although self-education had everything to do with it.

The owner of McGraw-Hill/Macmillan, a leading textbook publisher, and the owner of Berlitz, the world's premier language schools, was, himself, a grade school dropout. Is there, perhaps, a lesson in these stories? Would his products and services have been less appealing if his private history had been known?

◆

What we have most to fear is this: that school in the year 2090 will be exactly like school in the year 1990. As school in 1990 was exactly like school in 1890 except for cosmetic differences. But a century earlier, in 1790, it was still possible to get an education in the U.S. One dramatic evidence of that was that Tom Paine's *Common Sense* sold 600,000 copies in that year to a population of two and a quarter million, three-quarters of it slaves and indentured servants. Almost nobody has the *skill* to read *Common Sense* today, even though its language is simple and powerful.

In 1790 school didn't preempt all the time of the young in endless abstractions, nor did it act as the major destabilizer of family life then, nor did it disseminate a river of half-truths and state-approved myths so that its clientele were turned servile and mindless.

School in 1790 didn't drive children insane as it does today.

Alexis deTocqueville said in 1831 that the common people of America were the best educated in the history of the world. That was before we had a government monopoly in schooling — does anyone think he'd say that again?

Whether it's going to be possible to get an education in the schools of the year 2000 will depend on political decisions made by those who hold power in trust for all of us. Or it will depend on the defiant personal decisions of simple people like you and me. Like the quiet revolution that caused 600,000 American families to school their children at home, up from 10,000 families a decade ago.

◆

Our system of government schooling destroys both mind and character. It prevents the formation of the most precious resource of all — a self. To have a self you can trust it must be singular, it must be bold, it must be brave, resourceful, strong, self-reliant, unfettered. Does anyone in this audience think government schools teach these things? If you do you must be crazy. Perhaps you should teach in these places as I did for 26 years so you could know them inside out.

A school which educates cannot be a walled compound. It cannot employ a permanent priesthood certified as politically correct by the State and its economic partners like the teacher-colleges.

Why is Community School District 3 so very bad if it contains both a wealthy population — and Columbia Teachers College, the world-famous Bank Street College, and Fordham University School of Education inside its boundaries? The utter bankruptcy of teacher college education is found in the record of Community School District 3 over the past 23 years under Decentralization. Ask the colleges why this collection of schools is so bad. Listen carefully as they answer. Watch their eyes.

With the end of mass-compulsion schooling, corrupt relationships with universities peddling teacher credits, with publishers peddling useless texts, with building contractors (who are among the major supports of government schooling), and with other profiteers who thrive on a mass captive audience will cease.

The new school, if it happens, will eliminate testing as we know it because it does massive and permanent damage to children without producing any information of value — or even reliability. Testing as we have it is another profitable racket — ranking children through abstract measures with no verifiable connection to character traits we hope to cultivate in children — or any connection with developing mental powers. It is a rigged game and the testing industry is a gangster industry, which, through number magic, justified managing our citizenry as ancient Egypt managed its own — as if they distribute along a pyramidal hierarchy. They don't, that is what I've learned in 26 years of teaching rich and poor. And paper and pencil testing has no other use, it is a poor predictor of anything real.

The most disturbing instance of the testing racket is the multi-billion dollar reading remediation program. To learn to read fluently takes about 30 contact hours. It is a fairly easy skill for anyone to pick up, and millions know how to read *before* they go to school, having picked it up on their own.

Indeed, the only way to stop a child from reading and liking it in a literate environment is to teach it the way we teach it. But the industry of reading and its pseudo-scientific scare tactics is the most effective way to intimidate parents and taxpayers to stay in line, so you are discouraged from finding out just how easy it is.

So far, our new school has dropped walled compounds — its exercises occur everywhere: in offices, museums, companies, on farms, ships, in private homes, in churches, and in other rooms of a thousand types.

Our new school has decertified schoolteaching also, so that anyone with a skill to transmit can easily be put in touch with those who want the service. We have the technology to do this right now, all we lack is the will to deconstruct the empire of bad government schools we have erected over our children.

And most important of all, our new school has to put the money to purchase educational services back into the hands of taxpayers. It trusts itself to be able to win favor — and if it guesses wrong, it will have the decency to close up shop and go away. Government schools will compete with the others, but to win they will have to earn it. That would be a revolutionary change, wouldn't it?

The new school has flex-time, flex-space, flex curriculum, and flex-sequencing, because the range of human variety *demands* that; it has eliminated standardized testing — not because we don't need standards, we do — because standardization is the best way to assure the lowest possible quality of performance.

Time to stop the dishonesty. All of us are sickened by it, even those who *think* they profit by this system. We are dying as a nation and becoming a State. A nation is run by neighbors, but a state is run by experts. Monopoly schooling is a poison killing our nation. Don't look to schools for your salvation, *they have no idea what to do*. Look to your own courage, look to your own wits, look to your strong right arms. Demand free-market choice schools, help us get a school choice bill before the State legislatures.

Trust yourselves, trust the people, trust the kids. God bless you all in the struggle ahead. ◆

New York Teacher Of Year Calls For Free Education Choices

by Jeff Collins
Staff Reporter
Bellingham Herald

Calling for more free choices other than the current "public school monopoly," maverick education reformer John Taylor Gatto spoke to a receptive audience of more than 1,800 people at Bellingham High School Wednesday night.

The theme of Gatto's speech was entitled "The Hidden Curriculum of Compulsory Schooling." Gatto lashed out at school boards, teacher certification programs and government controlled schools.

A junior high school teacher for 30 years in New York, Gatto was named Teacher of the Year in New York City for three years from 1989 to 1991 and New York State Teacher of the Year for 1991. His book, *Dumbing Us Down: The Hidden Curriculum of Compulsory Schooling,* has been a best-seller in the Puget Sound Area since its publication in January. He has appeared on the "McNeil-Lehrer Report" and "Good Morning America." In 1984, he was the winner of the President's Volunteer Action medal for sponsoring 30,000 hours of volunteer work with young people.

Gatto said he's been busy on his West Coast trip to California, Oregon, and Washington. He's spoken to audiences, as well as holding a conference with Governor Booth Gardner, and lobbying for California's "Free Choice" bill. The "Free Choice" bill, a first in the country, allows public funds to go to more diverse systems of education.

Gatto began the almost three-hour discussion comparing the government handling of the water shortage in California to its handling of public schools.

"The real mission of large institutions, water boards, and schools alike, is to grow and thrive while using monopoly power to benefit its own managers and political friends," Gatto said.

The thrust of Gatto's speech was to allow free choice of public education by forcing the government to give up what he called its hold on public education.

"The word public in our form of public education has not had a real meaning for a long time," Gatto said. "Public schools will come back when we strip control from the certified expert class, and force our government to return free market choice to us," he added.

"The best way to offer real choice — soon — is to grant each public school the full freedom and independence private schools have. To desystematize them into neighborhood schools, with neighborhood directing boards and budgets."

Gatto expressed another one of his proposed resolutions by granting "each private, parochial and home school equal access to public funds. Almost all quality control in such a system will be provided by the market place. People will vote with feet and wallets…that would be a real public way of managing things."

He called for an "end to the teacher certificate monopoly. It makes colleges rich. It supports an army of unnecessary occupation titles." Adding that "certification itself is in too many cases the best evidence that a dependent and an unselective mind is present."

Much of Gatto's lecture approached the history of American education since its infancy in 1850. He called the experiment a failure.

"The real villain is an abstract idea, the theory that somehow the destiny of huge masses of people could be vested in the hands of the few," Gatto said.

In his speech, Gatto used competitive market analogies in his argument to free school systems.

"If I demand you to give your sewing machine to an anonymous repairman who needs work, you'd think I was crazy. If I came to your door with a cop who forced you to do it, forced you to pay the repair man, you'd be outraged," Gatto said.

Asking the audience, "Why are you so docile when you give your son or daughter to a government licensed teacher to work on? …You didn't choose your teachers."

The cost of bringing a child through the public school system in New York state costs about $168,000 each, when lost interest is calculated into the capital sum, Gatto said. In Washington state that cost runs just over $100,000.

"The source of this money isn't from some abstract entity called the government, it's from your sweat."

Gatto ended his speech by asking the audience to trust themselves to find answers to better education, saying "we've trusted the experts far too long." He left the stage to deafening applause.

The Curriculum Of Reform

An Afterword

By John Taylor Gatto

"In the space of one lifetime, the United States went from a place where human variety had room to express itself to being a laboratory of orthodoxy..."

The U.S. is a mirror revealing its builders and the shape of their souls. In the North American system men and women are subjected from childhood to an inexorable process of adaptation; certain principles contained in brief formulas are endlessly repeated by the press, radio, churches, and schools, and by those kindly sinister beings, the North American mothers and wives. A person imprisoned by these schemes is like a plant in a flower pot too small for it; he cannot grow or mature. This sort of conspiracy cannot help but provoke violent individual rebellions. Spontaneity avenges itself...

– Octavio Paz

Most of you, indeed, cannot but have been part and parcel of one of those huge, mechanical, educational machines, or mills, as they might more properly be called. They are, I believe, peculiar to our own time and country...

– Charles Francis Adams, Jr.

*I*n the space of one lifetime, the United States went from a place where human variety had room to express itself to being a laboratory of orthodoxy — a process concealed by the active maintenance of a mythology of independence. The cowboy and frontiersman survived into 1970 as living ghosts of some collective national aspiration, but both were dead in fact shortly after the Civil War.

The crucial years for the hardening of our national arteries were those between 1845 and 1920, the immigration years. Something subtler than Anglo-Saxon revulsion against Celt, Latin, and Slav was dynamically alive in those years and that something was a utopian ideal of society as an orderly social hive. This notion was not a new one, it had been transmitted continuously through elite bodies of men since at least the time of Hellenic Greece, but the New England colonies of the new world had been the principal proving ground of this ideal. There the idea had worked, generating wealth, stability, and order. Now it was to take advantage of the chaotic period of mass immigration — and the opportunity afforded by the Civil War to establish a uniform state.

The plan advanced like a disease, in stages, each new progression of state expansions making it more difficult for families to select their own destinies. Ultimately, in the same decade that gave us Adolf Hitler, Prohibition, mass IQ-testing of an entire population and world-wide depression, room to breathe in a personal, peculiar, idiosyncratic way just ran out and families were crushed. It was the end of Thomas Paine's dream, the betrayal of the democratic promise in the last possible new world of the planet, these states united by a utopian vision and yankee bayonets. Poe's "Pit and the Pendulum," where superheated metal walls of a prison cell close inexorably, forcing a captive toward the black abyss as his only escape, is an appropriate emblem for these 75 short years. It wouldn't be surprising if Poe had some glimpse of the future in mind when he wrote it.

◆

When you consider how bizarre and implausible much of the conformist machinery put in place during this critical period really was — and especially when you consider how long and successfully simple people resisted this kind of encroachment on fundamental liberty it becomes clear that to understand things like universal medical policing, standing armies and navies which demand constant tribute, universal military training, standardized national examinations, intelligence tests, compulsory education, secret national police forces, the organization of colleges around a scheme called "research" (which makes teaching an unpleasant inconvenience), the secularization of religion, the rise of specialist professional monopolies sanctioned by the state, the cult of total surveillance, and all the rest of the "progress" made in those 75 years, you are going to have to find reasons to explain

1) *Why* did it happen *then?*
2) *Who* made it happen?
3) *What* were they after?

2. An Extraordinary Vision

*I*t should be clear that no accidental convergence of historical forces caused the hive world to close in on us. The very clear social and hereditarian connection between all zones of the emerging American hive are a sign some organized intelligence is at work, with some special end in mind. For those who can read the language of conventional symbolism, the philosophical way under investigation here is elegantly represented on the back of our twentieth century dollar bill. It represents the extraordinary vision of the learned company of deists who created our national state.

Their own vision of democracy would be unrecognizable to most of us, just as the God in which they trusted was indisputably not the God of Christianity, but some great architect of the universe whose curious eye can be found both at the center of 17th century drawings of Solomon's Temple and at the top of the pyramid on our dollar bill, a fact I mention to emphasize how well-organized, self-aware, and purposeful this group really was. The eventual goal of their vision, perfected society, could only be achieved according to their blueprint when all human differences were reduced to a minimum and classified into rational hierarchies. In other words, when all men were either perfectly interchangeable, or perfectly subordinated, as are the stones of a pyramid, without complaint or competition. It is the Unitarian utopia I've just described, essentially a universe in which God and family are both superfluous, a world of "ethical culture."

The various ways this ancient ideal can be given life through institutions under control of the State are often subtle, but one of them is so startling, and has been realized so closely, it bears comment. As the hive-world was being hammered out after the mid-19th century, the notion of unique, irreplaceable natural families came increasingly to be seen as the major roadblock in the path being socially engineered toward the extraordinary vision of our utopian founding fathers. The way to remove this roadblock was to establish national consensus that all families should be "conditional." That is to say, families should be *on trial* with each other and with their neighbors, just as a politician is on trial with his constituency. If, after a test period, an "original" mother and father did not suit the standard of parenting established by a professional class of experts, then children should be removed and transferred to better parent surrogates. By 1900, Children's Court, the machine intended to perform the transfer function, was in place. Children need no longer be wasted building blocks for the State just because their natural parents had been so. The lesson the new machine-economy was teaching was very unlike the interdependent-family lesson of agriculture, it reinforced the congregational vision of the utopians, independence, not interdependence. Perfect interchangeability, perfect subordination. No complaints, no envy. The harmony of technology was a daily inspiration in building toward the new secular order.

Similarly, husbands and wives were encouraged through easy divorce laws and easier access to sexually explicit imagery, to be selective about choosing marriage mates. The new system encouraged several trials — trying on different mates until a good fit was found. Psychic difficulties brought about by this rationalization of a complex phenomenon were regarded as friction in a machine, trouble could be oiled away by adjustment therapies administered by a state-licensed professional class.

◆

Historically speaking, the mechanistic utopian jacket being cut to fit Uncle Sam in the second half of the 19th century had been designed in two astonishingly influential regions of European prehistory — ancient Athens and the Nordic rim of Europe in Viking times. Both these lightly populated but once dominant political arenas depended for their prosperity on fighting ships powered by oars. Although popular imagination associates such technology with the Vikings, the Athenians were equally dependent on the rowing skill of disciplined crews to establish a masterful relationship with neighboring states.

The lessons learned in rowing fighting ships, blended into the shape of utopian vision, passed down through history from these places. And the lessons are so inherently antagonistic to healthy *families*, it is no wonder that history's only purely utopian experiment in statecraft — the United States — took the anti-family direction it did. Harmony-through-variety is the way successful families organize themselves, but the same practice would spell suicide on a fighting ship where the greatest standardization of physical movement must be achieved. Living rowers in battle must be able to instantly accommodate the dead in their midst and adjust without losing a beat because of sentiment. Even the most proficient quickly realize their own survival depends on the worst rowers being very much like the best. Fighting such a ship demands the closest surveillance of comrades, a ruthless ability to dispense with the weak, and an automatic quality of self-discipline.

In that dynamic 75-year space between 1845 and 1920 the American political and social apparatus came increasingly to be viewed by a partially invisible intellectual elite as a fighting ship powered by oars. It had a course, a destiny — not just a present position that could be fixed by coordinates. And this course should not be left subject to accidents of wind, but should be under the control of a captain whose purpose was uniform with their own.

Not everyone was disciplined and skillful enough a rower to be invited to look at the sailing charts, but that such maps existed is evidenced by the back of the dollar bill as well as the anti-family consistency of our institutional logic. Each passing decade made the plan of total intervention into every individual life and every family life abundantly clear.

Protests were of course raised, but they became feebler with time. No room existed for the luxury of a stupid sentimentality, any more than such room exists on a fighting ship. The subtitle of Darwin's 1859 guidebook to the new order, *Origin of Species* is seldom mentioned these days, but remains sharply instructive, "The Preservation of Favoured Races."

Only fools believe favored races owed unfavored ones anything except extinction and slavery — despite the injunctions of Christianity — but an ethic of fairness was not completely absent. To correct any mistakes of brute Nature this principle was offered: If a man from an unfavored race was willing to surrender his inferior culture and to be as we are (in the words of the Know-Nothing Party) then he would be welcome to participate in the new secular order. Christianity was dying rapidly in 19th century America, but rational scientific orthodoxy moved into position as a spiritual substitute. The brand-new culture of universities and compulsory schooling, Chataquas and centralized exhortations were to serve as the new Ark of the Covenant.

And woe to those who would resist. The unprecedented Massachusetts Adoption Law of 1851 made it clear this would be a no-holds-barred fight to the death against deviants.

3. Saxon Attitudes

*I*s it really necessary to go back to Luther's Saxony and beyond to find the fountainhead of American Orthodoxy? Yes. Theologically the American nation was, on the surface at least, a Protestant experiment. Two hundred and thirty-three years after Jamestown the U.S. had a population of just 25,000 Catholics, half of those in Maryland, and only a handful of Jews, almost all Sephardim. Every developed, or developing embryonic institution was a reflection one way or another of what Luther seeded in Saxony in the early 16th century.

On a matter as important as this assertion that antique religion acted as a handmaiden for our technological orthodoxy you'll want some reassurance. Thomas Huxley, who more than any other man created and merchandised Charles Darwin, will provide it for you. Huxley himself was a thorough-going atheist yet when it came to definitions of right thinking, Huxley's mind turned naturally to Reformation images. In the following citation the incestuous connection between "outmoded" theology and "objective" modern science, in Huxley's mind at least, dances nimbly upstage:

> "The doctrines of predestination; of original sin; of the innate depravity of man and the evil fate of the greater part of the race; of the primacy of Satan in his world; of the essential vileness of matter; of a malevolent Demiurgus...faulty as they are, appear to me to be vastly nearer the truth than the liberal popular illusions that all babies are born good..."

◆

As you will understand, when the scientific establishment regards good babies as popular illusion quite a can of worms is thereby opened.

Huxley wrote that in 1892 — which really isn't very far away. I feel its hot breath on my neck as I write. Luther's Saxony. As fascinating as Luther himself. Where the new reverence for riches and power first crystallized after gradual evolution between the 14th and 16th centuries. *It was in Luther's Saxony where clocks were first set to strike the quarter-hour instead of hourly. A reminder that time was flying, not to be wasted.* It is worth dwelling a bit on those clocks and what the regulation of *time* signifies and portends.

Time is seldom regular. Consider how time feels in the grip of passion against the feeling it engenders when standing in line at a supermarket cash register. Among the many things the Saxon system can be said to mean, it means at least this: That one hour is very much like any other. Interchangeable, when not subordinated into an impersonal orthodox arrangement like a 9 – 5 workday or schoolday.

Luther made a great many direct statements about orthodoxy which have insinuated themselves into our attitudes and institutions. Once he said:

> "Even if those of authority are evil or without faith, nevertheless the authority and power is good and from God. There-

fore where there is power and where it flourishes...it remains because God ordained it."

◆

Luther understood that *dissent* in orthodox systems is a cancer. Let one man refuse to row the boat as he is told — and get away with it — and the longship is doomed. Constant surveillance is necessary. An intimidating police power is necessary. Obedience is necessary.

Luther is candid in describing procedures needed to resist challenges to the social order

"Therefore let everyone who can, smite, slay and stab secretly or openly, remembering that nothing can be more poisonous, hurtful or devilish than a rebel...if you do not strike him he will strike you...one must kill a mad dog."

◆

By 1885 the standard method to deal with crowds which refused to disperse was to call out the militia, contingents of the Federal army, or private armed legions like the Pinkertons. These were then issued orders to smite, slay or stab secretly or openly, killing as many mad dogs as necessary to control the remainder.[1] Luther provided what appeared to be Christian sanctions for removing independent choice from the underclasses, even in cases where just grievances might exist. God chose, he said, "to suffer the government no matter how evil rather than allow the rabble to riot, no matter how justified."

The evolving American utopia took these lessons to heart. Temporarily, however, they had to be applied with discretion. Three factors dictated caution. First was the seemingly endless extent of the wide-open spaces. Next was the all-important secret war with Catholic Spain which took nearly total concentration to prosecute during the first half of the 19th century. And finally there was the inconvenient and dangerous philosophical split between the North and the South (as there has always been in Anglo/Teutonic affairs).

Behind the window-dressing of slavery lay the real contretemps. That was nothing less than the once personal decision just how important a man's family, friends, and community should be when balanced against his own material improvement and fame. The Old Norse Religion contended starkly that "word-fame" was bedrock human reality, everything else dies. *Somehow a continuity of this old pagan principle had*

---

[1] A horrifying example of this principle of cutting behavior to fit with bayonets has, not surprisingly, been stricken from history books. In September of 1913, 9,000 miners and their families left John D. Rockefeller's company town of the

entered the life of the new country, but less so in the South where family and community tradition was considerably stronger than in the North.

Railroads "cured" our wide-open spaces in jig-time, removing that danger to utopian uniformity, the Lone Star and Bear Flag republics cured Spain of over a million square miles of prime land by the 1850's. And as for the South, Appomatox Court House made the contest between family philosophies an academic question. The way to utopia was at last clear.

4. The State as Parent

Beginning about 1840 a group known as the "Massachusetts School Committee" held a series of secret discussions involving many segments of New England political leadership. Stimulus for these discussions (often led by the famous Horace Mann) was the ongoing deterioration of family life that the corporatizing of agriculture was leaving in its wake. A peculiar sort of dependency and weakness thought to be caused by urbanization was spreading, the once idyllic American family situation seemed to be giving way to widespread industrial serfdom, novel forms of degradation and vice were appearing everywhere. It was frightening.

And yet, a great opportunity was at hand, too, these men agreed. Plato, Augustine, Erasmus, Luther, Calvin, Hobbes, Rousseau and a roster of other like names, sometimes referred to by the discussants as "The Order of the Quest," knew that without compulsory universal schooling the idiosyncratic family would never surrender its central hold on society, and it had to be destroyed as a sentimental haven

---

Colorado Fuel and Iron Company. The walkout was in protest against company surveillance and intervention into every aspect of family life.

Rockefeller imported shootists out of Texas, New Mexico and West Virginia and these were immediately deputized as Colorado lawmen. Rifle pits were dug into the hills around the striker tent colonies and equipped with machine guns, rifles and searchlights. The largest tent colony near Ludlow, Colorado was then attacked. Gunmen poured machine-gun and rifle fire into the tents for 12 hours. Rockefeller's army then entered the tent colony, pouring coal oil on the tents and setting them on fire. Women and children had sought refuge in pits beneath the tents and were baked alive. Nobody knows how many of these rebellious mad dogs were killed, but in one pit eleven children and two women were found burned to death.

Neither Rockefeller nor any of his men were ever charged with a crime by Colorado or Federal authorities.

before it could be pressed into the service of higher ideals — those of the perfected State. Perhaps this time of historical confusion could be capitalized upon to make this ancient dream a reality.

In a defensive mood, Mann saw that society's "guards and securities" had to increase because an unpredicted pathological phenomenon was following the introduction of machinery into life. The productive potency of the machine produced "artificial wants" and multiplied the temptation to have *things* — sometimes at any cost, indeed a new industry called advertising was orchestrating temptation. And the barbarous lives of the factory laborers made families a mockery; morality could no longer be taught by such parents.

Mann predicted crime and vice would explode unless children could be pried away from degraded custodians and civilized according to formulas laid down by the best minds and morals of New England.

Barnas Sears, Mann's colleague, soon to be number one man in New England education, saw the rapid growth of a commercial mass-entertainment business catering to the dense masses of urban humanity as "a current of sensuality" sweeping everything before it unless counterbalanced. Former bucolics who once looked to nature for their entertainment were pawns in the hands of wicked worldly wisemen. Urban confinement robbed simple people of the ability to find satisfactions outside the titillation of mechanical excitement. Whoever provided a desired succession of excitements would become the master of these half-men, it appeared.

Mann's other colleague George Boutwell (who would inherit the leadership of New England education after Sears) emphasized a course must quickly be selected from which there could be no turning back. Urbanization spelled the collapse of worker families. *There was no remedy.* Fathers were fatally diverted by non-agricultural labor from the custody and training of their children. Other claims of society and urban fashion led to neglect by mothers.

"As in some languages there is no word which expresses the true idea of home," said Boutwell, "so in our manufacturing towns there are many persons who know nothing of the reality."

◆

In words that might have been lifted from Anna Freud's 1972 treatise acclaiming stranger-adoption "in the best interests of the child," *Mann proclaimed that the State must assert itself as primary parent of the children.* If an infant's natural parents were removed — or if parental ability *failed* — it was the duty of government to step in and fill the parent's place. Mann noted that Massachusetts had a long tradition of being "parental in government." His friend, Sears, remarked that the State was a "nourishing mother, as wise as she is beneficent." Yet, should difficulties arise, the State might become stern — as befits a ruling *patriarch*.

5. A Little Nasty Medicine

*T*he most surprising thing about the start-up of mass public education in mid-19th century Massachusetts is how overwhelmingly parents of all classes rejected it. They fought against compulsions employed to secure and hold their children — until despair broke them; reports of school committees around 1850 show the greatest single theme of discussion was the conflict between government and the general public on this matter.

Resistance was led by the old yeoman class — those families accustomed to taking care of themselves and providing a meaning for their own lives. The little town of Barnstable on Cape Cod is exemplary. Its school committee lamented

"The great defect of our day is the absence of governing or controlling power on the part of parents and the consequent insubordination of children. *Our schools are rendered inefficient by the apathy of parents.*"

That passage is misleading at first look. The apathy and lack of control described was a direct reference to parental unwillingness to surrender their children to strangers for the balance of their youth; it was a formula well-understood by parents then to be tantamount to the destruction of close family life. General lack of parental interest in schools is an important theme in virtually every school report of the period.

But school committees represented minds far superior to those of parents, minds whose philosophical program was continuous back to Plato's *Republic*. And these committees were far from lily-livered; the demand for compulsory schooling, if not accepted willingly, *would be imposed*. The message to resisters never softened. It read: "Your children will be educated as we see fit."

◆

The first compulsory schooling in the modern era of the U.S. was a reform school movement. Know-Nothing legislatures of the 1850's saw to it this went into the hopper with their radical new adoption law. Objects of reformation were announced as

1) Respect for authority   2) Self-control
3) Self-discipline

The properly reformed boy "acquires a fixed character" and one that can be planned for in advance by authority in keeping with the dynamic needs of business and industry. Reform meant the total transformation of character through behavior modification. By 1857, six years after child-adoption was kicked off as a new policy of the State, Boutwell could consider foster parenting (the old designation for adoption) "one of the major strategies for the reform of youth."[2]

◆

The strategy of reform was for the State to become the actual parent of the child. That, according to another Massachusetts educator, Emory Washburn, "presents the State in her true relation of a parent seeking out her erring children."

The 1850's in Massachusetts marked the beginning of an epoch. Washburn triumphantly crowed that these years produced the first occasion in history "whereby a state in the character of a common parent has undertaken the high and sacred duty of rescuing and restoring her lost children...by the influence of the school." John Philbrick, Boston school superintendent, said of his growing empire in 1863, "Here is a real home!" All schooling including the reform variety was to be in imitation of the best "family system of organization." This squared with the prevalent belief that delinquency was not caused by external conditions — thus letting factory-owners off the hook — but by the internal lack of a "real home."

How institutional housing of delinquent boys gave way to *adoption* of the same boys grew out of a refinement of the same principle, to wit: "We shall find in our public institutions that...the nearer they approach the family system the better, and the contrary." But family units created at reform schools were too artificial. To obtain the full benefit of family experience the strategy of "reform" called for children to be placed "in the quiet circle of a New England family."

Between 1840 and 1860 male schoolteachers were abruptly cleared out of the Massachusetts system and replaced by women. A variety of stratagems were used, including the novel one of paying women slightly more than men in order to bring shame into play in chasing men. *Again, the move was part of a well-conceived strategy:*

"Experience teaches that these boys, many of whom never had a mother's affection...need the softening and refining influence which woman alone can give, and we have, wherever practicable, substituted female officers and teachers for those of the other sex."

[2] The reader will recall such a strategy was considered for Hester Prynne's child, Pearl, in Hawthorne's *Scarlet Letter*. That Hawthorne, writing at mid-century, chose this as a hinge for his characterization of the fallen woman Hester is surely no coincidence.

◆

Children committed to the extensive reform school system were often there according to a state report, because guardians, step-fathers, and natural parents sometimes tricked their children into committing "technical" offenses so they could be confined at the expense of the state! Another state report noted the *frequency* with which parents coming to collect their own children were met by the news their children had been given away to others through the state's *parens patriae* power.

"We have felt it to be our duty *generally* to decline giving them up to their parents and have placed as many of them as we could with farmers and mechanics," reads a portion of *Public Document 20* for the state of Massachusetts in 1864.

6. Getting the Children

*T*he inception of compulsion in schooling marks something more ominous than a simple *ad hoc* solution to problems of child care. Widespread opposition to this program, described brilliantly by Michael Katz in *The Irony of Early School Reform*, is evidence to arouse our suspicions that something else besides do-goodism was in the air. Remembering Boutwell's curious description of foster-parenting as "one of our major strategies" gives us a clue. Whatever was going on behind the scenes, its principals regarded their own position as that of military commanders, adapting tactics to fit a comprehensive plan.

The target was never less than whole categories of the population: industrial workers, professional men, and especially assemblies of immigrant labor. The *methodology* of reform was a set of adjustments, molds, social amputations, etc. which would cause targeted groups to be re-formed into useful tools to bring about the *curriculum* of reform. And that we already know is a state of society where abstract principles of justice reign, the particular kind of "justice" Plato described in his utopia. That form of justice is marked by the absence of families, the interchangeability of individuals in any particular class, and the perfect, willing subordination of all classes to the State.

◆

The power of this utopian scheme — for most of history an intellectual and psychological power — was brought to reality by the machinery of American technology which gave to it an economic dimension. While old complex Europe fiddled with mystical industrialists like Robert Owen and was burned by moralists like John Ruskin and Thomas Carlyle, American industry was being issued a blank check by the Civil War. Uniformity and regimentation were the golden keys to industrial fortune. *Anybody* who got his hands on cheap labor was able to get rich.

The new cash motivation to homogenize and subordinate men proved irresistible. So much money was made so fast by military suppliers mass-producing for the rigidly stratified mass armies assembled for the conflict that vast amounts were available to corrupt the politicians of the country on every level of government. With the fall of the South there was no opposition left of any magnitude, not even theological opposition. The Gospel of Wealth became the order of the day, old-line Protestants became "new wave" Unitarians, finally caving in to the deist vision of Jefferson reborn. But best of all, the entire male younger generation of the nation, North, South, East, West, had been trained for *four years* in perfect subordination. Perfect, willing subordination into military ranks where good soldiers follow orders even to death. On such a foundation, only a stone could not make money. The principle of interchangeability of men, and the perfect subordination of the classes to each other took a giant step forward.

An irresistible directorate was now primed to operate into the next century. The secret of successful opposition to any secular tradition is a relatively free childhood in which one may explore the world unmonitored. The self-knowledge and sure-footedness that result from such training spell trouble for systems requiring conformity. But uniqueness can't develop in the collective stiffness of a school setting, an open dormitory, a factory, or in any parliamentary team arrangement where young people are constrained to run together in like-age cohorts to the exclusion of any other grouping.

Individuality, as a function of distinctness, requires some solitary time and place to develop. It is aided powerfully, too, by access to companions who are themselves distinct and different by virtue of different ages and circumstances. The alternation of safe solitudes and equally safe convivialities that a loving family provides is the only reliable forge life offers in which identity, personality, unity, integrity, wholeness and vitality can be cast.

The vulnerability of human beings during family time came to be well understood by central planners in the middle of the 19th century. Whoever won the right to cultivate the young plants would have the harvest. Many elites clamored for this privilege: cultural purists, theologians, politicians and industrialists among them. But most consistent and effective were small, socially intimate intellectual elites who could trace their spiritual line in a continuum from Plato. And who could inspire themselves by considering the record of steady progress their brotherhood had made in every age. Although I've written as though these men were formally organized, and though I believe in some queer fashion they indeed were, even an informal association of influential men who shared the same view of the future would probably produce similar effects.

The strongest tradition of these elites was invisibility, the low profile. Like the unseen creature in Bierce's "Damned Thing," their passage through events is best marked by changes left behind. Sudden, swift alterations of what was once familiar landscape. Many of these alterations were spectacular like the rabbit-out-of-the-hat appearance of a U.S. hospital industry in the late 19th century, of the slambang transmutation of children's books into stories which took place in a world devoid of parents.

7. The Pagan Bible

*T*he indispensable utopia is Plato's *Republic*.[3] All Plato is a footnote to the *Republic* — it is the perfected utopia showing perfect justice to be harmony among all parts of society. Those who are subordinate accept their subordination willingly. The leadership can be said to create the moral world of simpler folk lying to them when necessary as a kind of beneficent oil to assist operations of the State.

The family is openly regarded as an enemy. Everything is where it ought to be. The best and brightest are at the top. It is a world going nowhere; it has already arrived.

Ask the question who reads Plato's *Republic* then and now and you get the surprising answer that everybody who counts did and does.[4] The majority of elite young college men in the past three centuries all read it. Other classics come and go, the *Republic* stays. It is on sale in every American bookstore. On the shelves of every single library, even the collections in tiny towns. The continuity of this pagan bible in west-

---

[3] Bertrand Russell raised a few eyebrows in 1920 when he announced that a close inspection of the new Russian Bolshevik state would reveal its theoretical substructure to be identical with that of Plato's *Republic* — and almost certainly stolen from there!

[4] According to biographers of the Ayatollah Ruhollah Khomeini, his vision of an Islamic state led by a philosopher-king stemmed from his time in Qum as a young man when he became enchanted by Plato's *Republic;* a recent display ad in *The New York Times* for Adelphi University announced that "everyone" should read Plato's *Republic* before entering college.

ern tradition has no peer at all unless it is the Christian *Bible*, which is hardly read at all.

Delving into this phenomenon, the situation discloses further strangeness. The Christian Bible is filled with fantastic tales, Oriental color, vivid language and images. Even in its decline the narratives are kept alive by tens of thousands of ritual assemblies each week. Great cinematic and televised adventures from the Testaments have been popular entertainment for over half a century. The great national celebration is Christ's birthday.

The pagan bible seemingly has no advantages. Plato gives us a group of men dressed in sheets who sit around talking about ideas. No action, the drama is eventless, and the republic being discussed is imaginary: How can we account for the fact this dull book's ideas have been continuously taught over a vast area for two thousand years and more?

Something had kept the *Republic* and its antifamily message vigorously alive while Hesiod, Cicero, Marlowe, Luther, Calvin, Newton, Darwin and Einstein turned to stone. Even the *merit* of its ideas is vigorously debated by teachers and classes — there is no consensus. No consensus, that is, except about one thing and that is the universal fascination *with the book's nature as a comprehensive secular agenda to organize all human society.* No other agenda besides Plato's has ever caught public imagination for more than a short time, or perhaps it would be fairer to say no other agenda has ever been assisted so mightily to extend very far beyond the lifetime of its creator.

8. Standardizing Deviants

The history of utopian writing after Plato shows plainly how impossible it has been *to even think of a social design not involving more state control.* The only important thing added, by writers after Plato to the idea of utopia is gadgetry, and every piece of that is designed to give the state greater control and surveillance capabilities. The philosophical climate is always one of *sanitary distance between rulers and ruled,* augmented by an atmosphere of illusion in these exercises.

When we come to consider just what might comprise an alternative to Plato the obvious antipode that suggests itself is the riotous choice of the natural world. We might expect to find common variations on naturalistic creeds opposing the religion of man-made rules and confinements. But this is not the case. Just as the printing press was making rapid dissemination of different points of view possible, these points of view, most violently antithetical to Plato's, were virtually abandoned!

Beginning in Britain about the year 1500 and continuing outward from there across much of the world for the next 500 years there has been a march toward seeing Nature as either inimical or exploitable. The Trevelyan Lectures of Keith Thomas in 1979 explain the catastrophic extent of this transformation from nature benign to nature malign. A utilitarian perspective gradually dominated, even theology was bent to its logic, with the settling of America a multiform, polychromatic situation once again prevailed temporarily in places until the 1840's, but after that Plato's agenda crept relentlessly over the landscape again.

◆

Platonic goals were always abstract, extrinsic to human nature as commonly understood and strongly antagonistic to individual variation. Such goals stress the needs of society and the economy: "Ask not what your country can do for you, but what you can do for your country," was John F. Kennedy's platonic exhortation at his inauguration.

Platonic goals can always be quantified, platonic citizenship can be interpreted statistically so it is predictable. School, for instance, may be justified by assigning a specific cash value to its duration. Even when actual evidence contradicts that human satisfaction can be measured by numbers — how big a bank balance? how short a work day? — people are conditioned to ignore their own primary experience — what they glimpse behind the noisy imprecations of social drillmasters.

Platonic goals are indifferent to human aspirations or indigenous cultures, and platonic reforms are imposed in the absence of popular acceptance as public education was imposed. Some leaders mount aggressive public information campaigns to sell new rules, other leaders cajole, using dramatic models of superior people accepting whatever new system is being forwarded for the moment. Outright deception and lies are allowable if other tools fail. And force is the antidote to resistance.

9. Inhuman is Best

The estrangement of the political system from human values is expected in a Platonic republic. Sophisticated men hardly bother to deplore it. Resistance is met by increasing the dose. A fascinating example of this principle is playing itself out now in the last fraction of the twentieth century in regard to the public schooling phenomenon.

Few institutions are considered so universally to have failed as our schools, yet in spite of this dreary record a prescription of increased dosage is making its way to the national agenda. The specifics of this proposal:

a) Schools should be open year-round, avoiding long summer holidays for children.

b) Schools should extend from 9 to 5, not dismissing students in mid-afternoon as is currently the case.

c) Schools should provide recreation, evening meals, and a variety of family services so that working-class parents will be free of the "burden" of their own children.

◆

The bottom line of these proposals is reduction of the damaging effects of "freedom" and "family" on a subject population.

Realization of this design would certainly be among the very worst things that could happen to our already crippled young. Yet it is not hard to see how logical a next step this is in approaching the total state of Plato's utopia. It is hard to think of a single such advance thwarted in the past 150 years, the movement has been so inexorable. All signs and portents say the comprehensive school plan will come to pass.

10. Reform as Magic

Reform is a concept most central to utopian thinking. All utopias spring from a desire to escape the world as it is — that is self-evident. But more is at stake than that; the techniques of reform are a species of magic intended to change natural reality.

Utopias are blueprints for change. Bit by bit they become the inspiration for the architecture of statecraft.[5] In the absence of other continuous blueprints it is only natural that they do this since dissatisfaction is endemic to human societies.

When the radical course of utopia is followed as it has been in our time by Roosevelt, Hitler, Stalin and many other smaller men, what must be involved is a violently abstracted perspective — seeing man and his world from a position outside man. A system can then be devised and each man ordered to fit the system as Procrustes ordered his victims to fit the bed by stretching or cutting them to suit. Everyone who lives under such regulation is partially dehumanized. Utopian thinking allows a strange feeling of dispassionate "objectivity" to pervade the arena of life; it makes opposition very hard to organize or maintain since even obvious victims of such social discipline have a difficult time explaining what is wrong.

Furthermore, systematic states have an answer to everything. Sys-

---

[5] Machiavelli saw that any systematic agenda will eventually be adopted if no competing agenda opposes it, regardless of its popularity.

tematic philosophy means never being caught with your pants down even when you are — all "mistakes" are "honest" mistakes. And systematic philosophies come equipped with contingency plans which bail them out of the worst messes they make; a striking example of this phenomenon in our own century involves the warrior states of Germany and Japan. Both these entities were seemingly pulverized by warfare, defeat, enemy occupation, and profound antagonism on the part of neighboring states. Yet both recovered and prospered a mere 20 years after their seeming destruction. The explanation lies in the fact each state understood its own value so clearly it was able to successfully intimidate victor nations into paying exceedingly large reparations for the privilege of winning! Tears for the dead or shame were clearly recognized by the systematic philosophy of both states as sentimental tomfoolery; the strength of Platonic logic in warfare is that individuals and families are of no consequence, both are easily replaced. This disinclination to mourn is a great advantage wherever score is kept materially. Both Germany and Japan were wonderfully invigorated by warfare — like men well-exercised. They had no difficulty returning to the serious business of making money.

It seems fairly clear that faced with the prospect of devising a systematic philosophy or borrowing one already around, more statesmen will follow the second course than the first. Thus it is no surprise that serious utopian writing has always found its audience in the corridors of government.

11. Novus Ordo Seclorum

*I*n Hertzler's *History of Utopian Thought,* the influence of Bacon's *New Atlantis* is traced. Hertzler makes a convincing case (from the testimony of its founders) that the Royal Society itself was due to the prophetic scheme of Salomon's House or The College of the Six Days Work in *New Atlantis*. Salomon's House is a world university assembling only the best under its protection. The book had immense influence in Italy and France, and in France it is considered the principal inspiration of the *Encyclopedia*. The connection of the French *Encyclopedia* to the American Revolution is a close one, has been told too many times to bear repeating. Suffice it to say the very same triangle-encased eye appears in early 18th century French drawings as appears on the back of the American dollar, and curiously enough it appeared on a private tract published in 1810 by an ancestor of the two Roosevelt presidents, a tract urging the total regimentation of the U.S. population.

◆

The biblical Solomon and Plato both concurred in thinking there was only one right way to do things. Both men have a powerful influence on western political life, and on other utopian thinkers like Charles Darwin. Darwin's notion that life is a contest in which the inferior perish offended the majority of Americans when it was published in 1859. And the grounds of attack were much broader than simply the field of religion; a number of critics recognized that this so-called theory was beyond proof or disproof and in fact constituted a massive piece of elitist rhetoric, quite theologically familiar in its allegations. Darwin's theory was rejected by a cross-section of Americans as they had rejected the notion of compulsory public schooling; this fact is reflected in state legislation well into the 20th century, so recently as 1989 California education authorities felt the necessity to order the teaching of evolution as fact, not *theory.*

School curricula have never been a matter of democratic choice; biology teachers almost everywhere were ordered by administrators to teach the evolution theory as fact and that is still the case today. The teaching of biology in public schools has been without doubt a major factor in gaining Darwin's position supremacy.

Here we are face to face with the naked mechanism of social engineering. Under no stretch of the imagination can biology teachers actually be deemed "scientists" — they undertake no original experimentation, record no original observations, and publish no discoveries, they are generally compelled just about everywhere to support whatever view the available textbook supports. This makes them pitchmen in scientific drag. Yet Darwin's utopian/dystopian rhetoric was spread efficiently by a fifth column of teachers positioned at key junctures on the youthline.

12. Dismembering Human Associations

One of the consistent goals of utopian procedure is a *detachment* of its subjects from partisan human enthusiasms. Acting with detached intelligence is what utopias are all about. But a biological puzzle intrudes: detaching intelligence from emotional life is tantamount to killing the natural organism. The feat has never been actually performed in physical terms although imaginative writers have been endlessly intrigued by the challenge. Poe's tale of Moxon's chessplayer, *Donovan's Brain,* and Odin's ravens come to mind. The psychoanalytic concept of alienation describes the common pathologies we associate with "detachment" of this fashion.

All serious attempts to create utopia must involve states in isolation or semi-isolation as the U.S. was in isolation until the mid-19th century (and as the Scandinavian countries have always been.) Utopian thinking despises variety and competition. In this regard the tendency of utopians to enlarge their canvas to include the whole planet is provocative. Utopians regard national sovereignty as irrational, sentimental clap-trap. Businessmen get richest when they swim in the world-economy, not alone in their native system, and reason would seem to hold that analogy true for world-personalities as opposed to legal ones.

To the utopian mind democracy is a polluting disease. We need one world and that one world should reasonably be under the direction of an elite, as Plato describes an elite in his class of Guardians. Democracy degrades the hierarchy necessary to operate a logical republic. Our own political parties retain only the merest notion of this idea, of course, but for all the congruency of our two parties, the democracy/republic combat takes place silently at the heart of each. But true republican thinkers allow themselves, ethically, the stratagem of employing *the illusion* of democracy because it delights the ignorant and confounds opposition.

An interesting aspect of nearly all utopias since the 16th century has been their addiction to inhuman machinery in place of human affection as the goal of a satisfying life. Often the visions of mechanical marvels to come have been uncanny in their precision, sometimes it seems that to think about a thing is tantamount to soon having it. A sort of Aladdin's Lamp exists in this regard in utopian fiction. There is a legend that in the lost Atlantis stood a great university in which originated most of the arts and sciences of the present world — it was in the form of an immense pyramid with a flat top from which star observations were made. Putting aside that pleasant fancy reminiscent of the art work on our dollar, almost any early utopia seems to have a profusion of inside information about things to come.

In 1641 Bishop John Wilkins, a founder of the Royal Society, brought out his utopia, *Mercury: or the Secret and Swift Messenger.* Every single invention Wilkins imagines in it has come about: "a flying chariot," "a trunk or hollow pipe that shall preserve the voice entirely," a code for communicating by means of noise-makers, etc.

Giphantia, written in 1760 by de la Roche, unmistakably invents the telephone, the radio, television, and dehydrated foods and drinks. Even the mechanisms suggested are the actual ones eventually employed.

McLuhan provocatively called upon us to notice that all machines are extensions of the human body and nervous system. And that their use amputates the natural part. They seek to improve on the natural apparatus, each a miniature utopianization of some function. But equally important is the effect — their use causes the natural flesh and blood analogue to atrophy.

Machines dehumanize men wherever they are used and however sensible their use appears. In a correctly conceived Christian demonology the Devil would be perceived as a machine. Yet the powerful, pervasive influence of utopian reform thinking on the design of modern states has brought utopian mechanization of all human functions into the deliberations of statecraft.

An important part of the virulent, sustained attack launched against family institutions of the United States 150 years ago arose from the need of utopians to escape fleshly reality. *Almost all utopian reformers since Plato have been childless.* When the obituary of family life is finally written definitively, forgive me for expecting its author to be somebody who didn't like his own family very much.

◆

"Hurrah for reform!" shouted Charles Loring Brace, accounted the chief architect of American stranger-adoption and the "baby trains" that put up children on western auction blocks to be reared by proper strangers.

13. Utopian Promises

The extent to which our part of the new world began as and has continued to be a practicing utopia controlled the shape of our institutions, the national agenda, and the development of a national mass-confusion-psychosis attendant upon this plan going unannounced and hiding behind the mask of democracy. U.S. family policy is still deformed, but relentlessly approaches the ideal utopian state of Plato's dream.

There is something chastening about suspecting the nation you think of as home. The minute you begin to doubt surface reality the possibility must be faced that you yourself may not be real. In a study of hundreds of grown-up adoptees in Canada the most common report among the group was the feeling, "I am not real." "I am not real," echoed Betty Jean Lifton, author and adoptee, in one of her books.

◆

There is no room anymore for families in our republic except on television and the unreality of the American utopia is becoming unbearable. Thousands of rich American teenagers kill themselves each year because of that fact and millions drug themselves into forgetfulness. When "kids" examine the passion they feel inside and then compare it with sterile adult lives about them, the certainty of such a fate descending is too much to bear, a real death is preferable to an unreal life stretching endlessly down the road. For those who survive to become adults, a kind of death-in-life is the norm. Shallow commitments mark everything: marriage, family, career, interests, friendships, religion. Flat emotional response is the safest way to survive in utopia.

◆

Children discover early that the totality of the adult world is woven out of utopian lies, while at one and the same time they are at that juncture of life when emotional truth is most valued. To make decisions based on illusion is deadly when you are young. There is no recovery from it. But instead of truth, betrayal after betrayal of truth is experienced.

Darwin was wrong. Those children with most natural genius for truth are those killed off first by the illusions of utopia. They make dramatic wreckage. The fittest to be human have the least resistance to inhumanity. It is the unfit children who survive the barrage of deceits, growing to appear perfectly normal while inside they flop about gasping like suffocating fish on the deck of a shallow-net trawler. Hiding from commitment. Plagued by the feeling they are not real.

They are correct. *It is impossible to be real without lines of binding commitment* to wives, families, work, the land — to some enduring part of the mystery. No one, however, is committed to utopia — at best they are "detached."

"Pretending!" "Pretending!" "I'm sick of lies!" I heard an adopted young woman shriek in a Manhattan church last month. "Was I born or adopted?," Leslie Chappell, a Vancouver adoptee who went to court and had himself legally un-adopted, wrote to me.

14. The Telling of Truth

When utopia failed to materialize in reality after the first world war, the national response, in keeping with America's tenacious English bulldog character, has been to try harder. It is high time we stopped and took another look at what is really wrong. Our families aren't dying, *they are being killed,* quite a different matter.

There are more synonyms for the concept of deceit in the English language than for any other single idea. Does that tell you something about how often dishonesty crosses the Anglo/American mind? And how important Plato has been in the formation of our unconscious national character? We have been tricked into building and maintaining an inhuman hive-society. If we cannot *persuade* new generations to accept this awful path we reserve the right to intimidate, deceive, contrive, fake, sham, pretend, flimflam, misrepresent, dupe, hype, trick, humbug, bluff, gammon, rook cozen, gull, and so on.

Regimentation, methodization, systematization, standardization, organization, coordination, disciplined arrangements, conformity — these things are at the very heart of our national state policies, and are the poison that has killed our families and left individual survivors in a numbed, angry, nearly hysterical condition. Its impossible to point the finger at one or another of our institutions to find a target for our wrath — all of them work on a cantilever principle of interlocking directorates now. You can't get a handle on any one of them like child care or stranger adoption without first fashioning a hypothesis about what is making all of them tick. What is the *destination* of their collective movement?

◆

The deeper I look in the history of an America unable to produce a sane family policy the more I come to see this failure as a byproduct of a comprehensive utopian plan — the standardization of deviant parts of the population by eliminating natural family life and replacing it with synthetic family life. I see a coherent, age-old unity — not all-powerful yet, but stronger every decade — advancing pseudopodia slowly, retracting them at times in the face of passionate opposition, but always flowing forward. Visions like that make you think you've taken leave of your senses.

15. Thomas Jefferson and Thomas Merton

*I*n 1801 Thomas Jefferson wrote to James Monroe, who had asked for advice about areas to which freed Negroes from the South could be removed. (In your innocence you may wonder why two presidents had to discuss where free men should be "removed," but these gentlemen were clearly thinking about a comprehensive plan for America's future, as were so many of the founding fathers.) Even in 1801 Jefferson was certain the slaves would soon be freed, but he was certain of something else, too. They belonged nowhere in North America or anywhere in South America either. In an anticipation of Darwin's *Descent of Man* he announced his fear of the effects of hybridization, speculating what "lack of purity" might do to the Anglo-Saxon race just as Darwin did 70 years later. In 1779 he had said "nature, habit, opinion, has drawn indelible lines of distinction between the two races. They cannot live in the same government."

By 1801, his fear of a free black population had significantly deepened:

However our *present* interest may restrain us within our own limits, it is impossible not to look forward to distant times when our rapid multiplication will expand itself beyond those limits and cover the whole northern, if not the southern continent, with a people speaking the same language, governed in similar forms...nor can we contemplate with satisfaction either blot or mixture on that surface.

◆

There is a right way and a wrong way, this language informs us. "Mixture" is the wrong way. 1801. In 1901, a hundred years later, a similar turn of mind, wonderfully pure even with the passage of years, would be used to handle Latin and Slav immigrants even as it handled redmen and blacks. Jefferson's orthodoxy comes at a surprising interval when all attention should have been directed to anticipation of the miracle of the new world. A world able to avoid the mistakes of the old, the repeated bloody attempts to force everyone to be alike. The exclusion of blacks can be seen as just another way to arrive at the same place, a notable failure of imagination in Jefferson. Once such a poison tree is growing only a hero would dare to cut it down.

◆

One hundred and fifty-nine years after Jefferson's letter to Monroe, a man named Thomas Merton emerged from a contemplative monastery to renew his contact with America. Long isolation often heightens perception of the familiar and enables us to see with fresh eyes. This happened to Merton. He wrote of what he saw happening after his retreat:

"In the last 20 years the world has moved a very long way toward conformism and passivity. So long a way that the distance is, to me, both frightening and disconcerting.

I have been all the more sensitive to it because I have spent this time in isolation. The America which I used to know as a rather articulate, critical and vociferously independent place...is certainly not so anymore.

Not that people do not complain and criticize, but their complaints and criticisms — indeed their most serious concerns — seem to be involved in trivialities and illusions, against a horrifying background of impending cosmic disaster."

He wrote that in 1960; the situation is considerably worse today. And the transformation accomplished by stealing children from their parents like some demoniac pied piper continues while closer and closer marches the total State dreamed of by childless Plato, a State without deviations, a unity, a perfect product of the curriculum of Reform. ◆

CARNEGIE HALL

1991-92 SEASON

Wednesday Evening, November 13, 1991, at 7:30

An Evening With

NEW YORK STATE TEACHER OF THE YEAR

JOHN TAYLOR GATTO

AND SEVEN OTHER VOICES OF SCHOOL REFORM

THE
EXHAUSTED
SCHOOL

THE ODYSSEUS GROUP

Group Odysseus takes its name and mission from the Greek hero who spent ten years fighting his way home, spurning wealth, fame, and the promise of immortality to reclaim his family. It is an appropriate way, we think, to target the role of government factory schooling in ruining American families, a role we hope to see ended. The experiment in social engineering which resulted in government compulsion schools in this country was unprecedented in Western history. In quick and violent stages between 1850 and 1920, agents of the State demanded the right to remove children from traditional ways of growing up, and the further right to confine these children in enormous compounds, segregating them by age so that they would be cut off from models of past and future, and ranking them according to measures which had little connection with realities of individual, family or community life.

Bertrand Russell called this "the most radical State act in human history," noting, in 1926, that the confined young people were being deliberately deprived of the tools of critical thinking. This was no accident, but part of a blueprint for a society in which the State would function as Mother and Father: a design first conceived in Plato's *Republic*, but passed to Horace Mann, principal architect of government compulsion schooling, by the Positivist movement in France. The new schools were intended to pre-empt the functions of families, teaching children to ignore both past (the Family) and future (self-reliance) because the State would make all decisions and serve *in loco parentis*. Children would also be made dependent on State schooling to generate the major lines of meaning and value in their lives.

Although the source of compulsion schooling's philosophy lies forgotten in the archives, like the mill that ground salt its anti-home, anti-family, anti-community traditions grind on, maintained in place by the school institution's "other" existence as the single largest jobs project in our society, and also as a major purchaser of goods and services. Vested interests which profit from schools as they are cannot school reform to shift resources from one place to another. All the engineering solutions needed to make schooling better were discovered long ago, the course of school reform lies in political solutions which shift control of the school dollar from bureaucrats and special interest groups to parents, neighborhood institutions, and local communities. The power to purchase the kinds of schooling that best fits each individual must be given back to the people.

The Odysseus Group stands apart from party politics. We aim to revive public discussion of education and give decision making back to the people. We hope to revitalize grassroots democracy by presenting a lively menu of successful working alternatives to government factory schools—some public, some private, some parochial, and some personal (the growth of homeschooling to encompass some 600,000 families and a million children nationally is one of the brightest chapters in our dismal school record). We intend to work toward legislative reforms which return school tax money to citizen hands where it can be spent to restore meaning to school choice by enlarging the range of available alternatives. We do not ask for an end to government schools, only that they be forced to compete. Free-market choice will improve government schools, too.

We need working partners, donors, advisers, correspondents, and volunteers. From Carnegie Hall we hope to move to a much larger forum and display many more successful working alternatives to the nation. If you can help, let us know. Odysseus finally made it home, so can we all if we are prepared to fight for it.

Meet the Speakers

John Taylor Gatto, 1991 New York State Teacher of the Year (and thrice named New York City Teacher of the Year by various organizations), had his teaching license terminated by School District 3 in 1986 while on medical leave of absence. He didn't find out he wasn't a teacher anymore until the beginning of the school year 1987, because the District "accidentally" sent notice of his firing to the wrong address. The charge was that he had abandoned his post. After nine months of unemployment a school secretary confessed that she had a copy of leave papers he had properly filed, and though the District complained bitterly that it didn't want him back, the Chancellor's Office reinstated him.

Six years earlier his wife Janet, Treasurer of the elected School Board of District 3, was accused in the press of signing checks for limousines, liquor, and other non-pedagogical items, and a major New York newspaper stated that she refused to answer questions about these checks. Since all of the checks in question were written while Janet and John were travelling in the Yucatan—and she had never been questioned about them by anybody prior to reading the press account—there was great puzzlement in the Gatto home, which deepened in the following week when the same great newspaper featured a headline: "School Board Treasurer *Admits* Signing Checks." (Emphasis added).

Such is the life of a public school teacher who looks upon government monopoly schools as psychopathic institutions, and tries to do something about them. The School Empire strikes back!

John Gatto is a Pennsylvanian from the Monongahela Valley, born on the spot where the first shots of the Whiskey Rebellion were fired 200 years ago by angry farmers deprived of their liberty by the new government. The rough Democracy of the Pittsburgh area, and its Scotch-Irish code of fierce independence, self-reliance, family loyalty, and distrust of government and abstractions marked his teaching from the first. "I recognized New York City schools for the ratholes they were right from the beginning," says Gatto, "but I decided to make a stand and take on a worthwhile purpose for my life. Our family motto is 'Sparkle and shine in the face of darkness' so I tried to do that twenty-seven years ago when I began teaching and I'm still trying."

His efforts gradually evolved into the famous "Guerrilla Curriculum" through which kids earn back their souls through a regimen of apprenticeships, independent study, field curriculum, work study, parent partnerships, solitary adventures, community service and interdisciplinary problem solving. "I teach them the dialectic, give then an experience base, and get out of their way. That's really all anybody needs. Ben Franklin and Andy Carnegie proved that." Over the years, the kids he taught enjoyed astonishing success, both in school and out, leading to the many awards this pistol champion, garlic farmer, author of five books, and nationally acclaimed lecturer has won. "They did it, not me. Remember that," he warns. "People do best when you stop teaching them and let them learn."

A professor of physics at Barnard College and Columbia University isn't supposed to run away to Boston, buy the old Nathaniel Bowditch mansion (The American Practical Navigator), and start a revolutionary private school, **Sudbury Valley School,** where kids are mixed together from the ages of five to eighteen, and where they teach themselves reading, writing, and arithmetic! But after two and a half decades of successful operation with kids from every walk of life—and a one hundred percent placement rate for every graduate who wanted to go to college—**Dan Greenberg** has just cause to feel proud as his Sudbury philosophy has become famous. Recently two Sudbury-model schools have opened in Oregon and more are on the way.

Married for over thirty years, this father of three children (and author of twelve books) rose swiftly in the academic world after his own graduation from Bronx High School of Science, taking his doctorate at Columbia in Physics at age 26. His first book, *Anaxagoras and the Birth of Physics*, was followed four years later with two more titles on the birth of scientific method and a guide to mathematics. Such credentials lend credibility to his dazzling assertion that Sudbury kids learn the entire elementary math curriculum in twenty contact hours, "some a little more, some a little less."

To see Sudbury Valley is to fall in love with it: the beautiful mansion, the stately lawn and trees, the lake and boathouse, the Victorian outbuildings, and everywhere kids engaged in graceful industry; debating school laws (in which they have an equal vote with Dan), baking brownies for a lunch hour business, reading peacefully by the lake, mixing together as though it didn't matter that one swing is occupied by a nine-year-old boy, one by a twelve-year-old girl, and one by a teacher!

Learning without coercion is a major theme of Sudbury, and the idea of personal respect for children leads almost directly to the concept of democracy as an institutional imperative. Everyone is involved in the full process of running the school, from hiring and contracting the teachers to passing on every school expenditure, penny by penny.

Perhaps the most revolutionary aspect of Sudbury Valley from a public policy aspect is that this graceful, fully equipped mansion with a 15,000 book library, magnificent shops, and low student-teacher ratio operates on much less than half the cost of a seat in New York City's degraded public school environment. How is Dan Greenberg able to do so much with so relatively little?

The key is the spirit of community which permeates the school. There is truly a spirit of commonality hovering over everything. Sudbury Valley has no "track" system, children with every conceivable interest exist side by side. They learn to cherish each other as human beings, and the friendships and bonds formed here remain strong for the rest of their lives, regardless of the professions they ultimately choose. Time assumes a different aspect at Sudbury Valley. Each student learns to understand and work with his own unique internal rhythm, pace, and speed. No one is a fast learner, no one a slow learner. All have in common the quest for a personal identity that is whole, and individual, and that, once found, makes all reference to time seem trivial."

—*Daniel A. Greenberg*

"The Exhausted School" takes pride in presenting a school like Sudbury Valley as counterpoint to the failure of government mass compulsion-schooling. The public interest would surely be served by listening to the experience of Dan Greenberg and adding a dose of Sudbury to the national school equation.

Pat Farenga, father of Lauren (five years old) and Alison (two years old) is one of the leading voices in American homeschooling—a phenomenon that has grown from 10,000 families a decade ago to 600,000 today. As publisher of *Growing Without Schooling*, as a speaker and writer, and as President of John Holt Associates in

Cambridge, Massachusetts, Pat is known from coast to coast as a worthy successor to his long time friend and mentor, the late John Holt.

Pat's mail-order catalogue for parents, children and others interested in learning outside of formal school systems has earned a worldwide reputation as both a witty and insightful information reference (Pat swears he writes it in the hot tub with Day), and a guide to the best work published about child-rearing. Nostalgically entitled *John Holt's Book and Music Store*, it regularly travels into thirty-five foreign countries as well as into every state. He is also a contributing editor to *Mothering Magazine*.

Pat Farenga's own keenest talent as a writer lies in ferreting out the myriad ways children learn that are unrecognized by most schools. His work emphasizes the astonishing educational value of real life, careful observation, playful imitation, apprenticeships, community service, and using the home as a base for self-directed learning. These are the primary ingredients in the pedagogy Farenga espouses.

Pat's unique experience as a central link in the burgeoning national homeschool network put him in great demand as a speaker for months in advance. Currently he is booked solid through June, 1992 when he will make appearances as various as The American Library Association Conference in San Francisco and the Libertarian Party Conference in Toledo.

Growing Without Schooling was founded in 1970 to support children's self-directed learning. There is no better way to gain a deep insight into the world of homeschooling than picking up a dozen back issues of this magazine.

What is in GWS as its fans call it? Letters from children:

After my mother and I talked and decided that it was stupid to go on hating math and not being able to use it easily, and that I was going back to straighten it all out—relearn the basic math skills. Mom and I went through our home library and got out all the workbooks and textbooks we could find, then spent some time working on them

together. Now I'm working on them myself.

At school it seems like they were trying to teach me things I already knew. Kids at school don't really like to read because they aren't allowed to read what they want. At home, reading is reading. We just read our books.

Letters from parents:

That year and the year before I was often very tired and often discouraged about home education. I'm so glad I didn't give up! Now the kids are happily learning at home!

Growing Without Schooling also interviews interesting thinkers and writers about education and parenting like MIT professor Seymour Papert:

The essence of what's wrong with school is this thing called instruction, and everything that goes with that: having people follow a curriculum, having them learn fragmented knowledge meted out in small pieces.

Each issue focuses on a specific topic or question, like learning by apprenticeship, children's rights, friendship, and every issue is jammed with information about the homeschooling movement. *Growing Without Schooling*, 2269 Massachusetts Ave., Cambridge, MA 02140.

 In the fifty-one years since **Mary Leue** graduated from Bryn Mawr in 1940, she's been a farmer in Maine, a registered nurse, a teacher, an editor, a writer, a publisher, a bookseller, a mother of five and grandmother of eleven, and dozens of other important things. But she is best known nationally and internationally as the founder of The Albany Free School, one of the longest running inner city independent

alternative schools in the nation, and as one of the leaders of the reborn libertarian school movement in the United States. Where many such schools came into being to serve upper middle class families and the wealthy, Mary firmly believed that open democratic education should be available to the children of the poor as well—and she set out to provide it in the city of Albany.

When she asked A.S. Neill, founder of Summerhill, what he thought about such a possibility he responded: "I would consider myself daft to try."

The immediate stimulus that drove her, however, was the distress of her own ten-year-old son who was suffering badly in the Albany public schools. She set about gathering a group of individuals and families who would join her in a vision of living, working, and studying in genuine community. Guided by the concept of work democracy, Mary and the Free School team began to create a series of small-scale community institutions to support the idea. She saw clearly from the start that her experiment would need its own internal economy, and would need to be based on true democratic leadership. It would need a strong philosophical base as well, drawn from many diverse traditions.

In 1969, with a handful of parents, the little school started up in what was then an Albany slum. Now, twenty-two years later, ten buildings are owned by the school (the money to purchase these earned by its own labors) and another ten buildings are associated with the school! In part because of the industry and beautification of Free School people and real estate, the neighborhood of the school is no longer considered a slum—and, indeed, looks something like the Georgetown area of Washington, D.C.!

What makes the Free School community an exciting and inspirational place is complex and unique, like any good community, but some of its working premises can be teased out for inspection. Prominent among these is the idea of total mutual support among all families in the school. That means everyone plays roles usually assigned to specialists, taking on more responsibility as a way of simplify-

ing the life of the community and making it as self-reliant as possible. Everyone teaches, and everyone rolls up his or her sleeves to help children and families in many other ways, too. We own a natural foods store, a bookstore, a custom boat-building business, a library, and much more—these group resources pay some of the costs of the school. Six years ago we set up a pooled investment group.

The school itself is far more a community center than it is a traditional institution, adults have as much fun as children in our school and staff burnout is unknown. Yes, our kids learn how to read, write, and do arithmetic—and they even go to college and take PhD's if they feel like it! But we manage without bureaucracy, taking any kid who applies, hiring any staff member who wants to be with us without checking for a state license to teach! Our internal economy, built from scratch, enables us to avoid the crippling dependency of government grants that limit the performance of many schools.

 Born in Knoxville, Tennessee, **Dave Lehman** took his doctorate degree at the University of Texas in Austin. Happily married with six children and three grandchildren, he has been teaching and working in education for thirty years, during which time he has founded both public and non-public alternative schools. He is presently the principal of Ithaca's Alternative Community School, a public alternative middle and high school. For his singular achievements he was recently awarded the title of "Outstanding Alternative Educator of the Year."

"We have options," says the former organic farmer, and writer on world religions and psychology, "for ways to study everything." Students and staff generate many of the curriculum offerings at IACS locally, in direct contradiction to the practice at customary factory schools of accepting orders from some central office far removed from the people involved in teaching and learning.

Dr. Lehman's own experience base is broad and deep, ranging from teaching biology in Ghana to being the basketball coach in Flossmoor, Illinois. He takes an active part in Ithaca community life, has been honored time and again with seats on various Boards of Directors, and publishes frequently in a range of journals including *Skole, Holistic Education Review, The American Biology Teacher, Phi Delta Kappan,* and *Colloquy.* He is frequently sought out as a speaker and consultant on curriculum, structure, and human relations aspects of schooling.

The chief industry of Ithaca, New York, is education, with Ivy League Cornell University its main employer followed by highly-rated Ithaca College and Cortland Community College, therefore it is a tribute to Dave Lehman's Alternative Community School that his own school's course offerings are frequently compared to college-level courses. Indeed seventy-five percent of his graduates go directly to college, even though the intake at IACS is an open enrollment type reflecting the ethnic and social diversity of Ithaca.

Some of the things that make the Alternative Community School different are these:

—Students receive narrative evaluations rather than grades, and this includes a self-evaluation section which gives them an opportunity to reflect on their own progress.

—Each student participates in three areas of school and self-governance: a small advising group of ten to fifteen students and one staff member meeting twice a week to work on school and personal issues; a twice a week committee meeting where students work on specific decision making bodies (i.e., Students Rights and Responsibilities, Review Board, Agenda Committee), or action-oriented groups (i.e., School Beautification, Cafeteria, etc.) and a once a week "Town Meeting" led by Agenda Committee members. Here the entire school community discusses and decides on pertinent all-school issues.

—Courses meet four times a week, not five, and students "elect" their courses from an array of offerings, all meeting State guidelines for academic require-

ments. There are also abundant opportunities for extended projects, independent studies, community studies (where students work closely with members of the Ithaca community), and study at other educational facilities, including Cornell, Cortland Community College and Ithaca High School.

Dr. Lehman looks at the school's "alternative" designation this way, "Isn't this what we all want?—the freedom to be fully our own selves in a community in which everyone else is, too? And in a place where we can all develop our unique potential?"

Roland Legiard-Laura learned the value of direct experience in eighth grade. "My history teacher asked someone to volunteer for military interrogation. The next thing I knew I was kneeling with my knee-caps on a broom handle!" The effect was profound, at once he understood the interrogation experience better than anyone could have explained. Since then the New York City born poet, building contractor, and filmmaker has opted for direct experience and the active role in life. Graduating with honors from Stuyvesant High, he delayed college and went off to Europe where he hauled grain on Dutch canal boats, learned Italian, studied fencing, and hitch-hiked across the continent four times. Returning to the U.S., he bicycled alone across the continent with a tire-repair kit that required sewing on the patches. "Fifteen flats later I knew I could handle anything."

Next came Hampshire College, where learning is entirely self-directed. He earned his degree there in 1975; his black belt in karate the same year. Back in New York he taught poetry in prisons and public schools as a CETA worker, then shortly thereafter founded "P.O.E.T.," a travelling poetry truck. The truck would strike targets of opportunity like bars, college campuses, and street corners where a dozen poets would leap from the vehicle without warning and declaim to the astonishment of all and sundry. In 1978 Legiardi-Laura and a few friends completely restored the Newsboys Lodging House on Tompkins Square Park as a residence. Hearing a rumor that Nicaragua's national sport was poetry, he made the first of four trips there in 1983 and decided to make a film about this culture hooked on poetry. Five years later he had produced "Azul" which, to date, has won nine international film awards including "Best Film" at the New York Documentary Festival. At one point during the filming he was ambushed with a platoon of soldiers but survived to see the same patrol reading poetry to each other an hour later.

In 1989, he became director of the Poet's Cafe, New York's only poetry nightclub and one of the hot spots of the downtown scene. Located in a five-story building renovated by Legiardi-Laura (over the years he became a building contractor as a result of learning each of the building crafts by trial and error), the Cafe has been featured in the press of 18 countries, most recently Japan. For the past two years Legiardi-Laura has been working on a major documentary film, *Teacher*, which uses his eighth grade English teacher, John Taylor Gatto, as a way of examining the culture of all schools, and exploring the art of pedagogy. Gatto and his students are more than subjects in this film, they serve as a medium through which profound questions are raised: Upon what philosophy is our system founded? What are its real intentions? What lessons are really taught in American schooling? What can be done to create a system consistent with our ideals? Perhaps as John Gatto says, the very idea of "systematic" schooling is itself the major problem. "Our children are dying in our classrooms," says Gatto, 1991 New York State Teacher of the Year. Why is it that a teacher of his stature and recognized ability rejects the system that has honored him?

Teacher will be the first comprehensive analysis of schooling ever filmed. "Funding a project of national scope like this is tough," says Roland, "New York's Council on the Arts just donated $20,000 and that means the work can continue, but we have a long way to go. We need support."

Helping hands, he promises, "will have a sonnet written in their honor."

In the "Sunshine" edition of the *Westside Teenage News* for April, 1980, this headline appears about **Barbara Jill (B.J.) Cummings**: "Teen Businesswoman Slams Board of Ed on Unrealistic Curriculum." The article quoted Miss Cummings as saying: "The business of America is business. That's what gives our society its particular style and flavor—then why do we learn so little about the inner workings of business, about jobs and economics? Bring us into office buildings and factories, show us how to start small businesses of our own. Teach us what we really need to know."

The article continued:

As the Board sat attentive, Miss Cummings exceeded the four-minute limit set for speakers as Stephen Aiello, President of the Board, waved her to continue. After twelve minutes she concluded. The Board rose as one in a long, standing ovation....

Eleven years ago as an eighth grader in John Gatto's "Lab School," B.J. Cummings made the long trip to the Brooklyn headquarters of the New York City Board of Education to protest the way government monopoly schools waste the time of children, hiding things from them they need to know. Now she appears at Carnegie Hall as a young UCLA doctoral student who taught herself Portuguese and travelled to the Amazon jungles alone at the age of 21 to examine the impact of dam-building on the native cultures above and below the dams. Funds were provided by The Explorer's Club and other institutional sources. The result was her compelling book, *Dam the Rivers, Damn The People*, credited in some circles as a major influence in halting the funding of Brazilian dams by North American banks! At a time of life when most young people just emerge into the grown-up world baffled, intimidated, and wondering what the future would hold, B.J. was already well along the road to making her own future.

She speaks of some of the risks of environmental study:

...while staying in a classic Amazonian frontier town with a Wild West flavor, I had spent the evening reading at one of the town's many bars. When it grew late and the bar became rowdy I returned to the home where I was staying. The following morning I took a walk through the town in the early light. Laid out on a table in front of the bar was the victim of a fatal blow to the head suffered in a brawl which had broken out after I retired the night before. No one was particularly concerned; it was a routine Saturday night.

Barbara Cummings, at age 24, has worked and studied in the rainforests of Panama, Brazil, Columbia, Australia, Hawaii, and on the African plains in Kenya. She had edited the national publications *Energy Review* and *Environmental Periodicals Bibliography*. Her first book, *Dam the Rivers, Damn the People*, recently released in England under the auspices of World Wildlife Fund, documents the Brazilian government's ill-conceived dam program on the Amazon.

She has served as a research assistant on a wildlife game reserve in Kenya, camped in the monkey forests along the Panama Canal, studied the flying foxes in the Queensland rain forests of Australia, worked for the U.S. Fish and Wildlife Department in Hawaii documenting the decline of forest birds, and is much sought after as a public speaker on environmental matters in this country and abroad.

Victor Gonzalez: "I originated in Puerto Rico and met Mr. Gatto thirteen years later. As you can see from the picture above I am a master of tight situations, but I hope someday to be a nationally famous writer and artist. With my partner Jamaal I've created Squadron Press, the owner of such amazing titles as *Ken Saki*—tales of a derelict Oriental New York City based Ninja. Mr. Gatto gave us a day a week to vanish to local libraries and graphic arts stores to find our own education. Ever since first grade I had a liking to making comic stories, and a talent for it that was discouraged by schools. But when I was turned down at a special art high school this year, my many grown-up artist friends went to bat for me and the school changed its mind. My most exciting moment so far was when I had breakfast with Debbie Winger and Senator Kerrey at the Algonquin Hotel and I got to sit on the arm of Miss Winger's chair and make eyes at her."

Jamaal M. Watson: "I probably got the most out of Mr. Gatto's Guerrilla Curriculum this year because, in addition to getting a day or two each week to work independently on my art with Victor, I won Congressman Rangel's citywide essay contest, first prize in a newspaper essay contest competing against high school kids from Stuyvesant and Bronx Science, and published an article in a national magazine. More than that, I got an apprenticeship with famous comic writer, Anne Nocenti (thanks Anne!), another with "Sesame Street" artist Nancy "Slim" Stevenson (thanks Slim!), and was accepted into a special high school.

In elementary school I was known as a big troublemaker; now I'm known as the creator of *Elvis Impersonator, Cracked City*, and as the finest short basketball player in America."